NUMEROLOGY
MADE PLAIN

REVISED *and* ENLARGED EDIT.ON

*The Science of Names and Numbers and
the Law of Vibration*

By ARIEL YVON TAYLOR

Author of "The Science of Numerology"

---

*" FORTUNE AND FAME ARE
IN YOUR NAME "*

LAIDLAW BROTHERS

TRADE DEPARTMENT

2001 Calumet Ave.   36 West 24th St.
CHICAGO   NEW YORK

TO

 EDNA PURDY WALSH

AN INSPIRATION FOR LARGER ACHIEVEMENT
TO ALL WITHIN THE REACH OF HER
PEN OR THE RADIUS OF HER
PERSONALITY.

CONTENTS

v

FIFTH EDITION GREETING

The new outlook on life which has come to many through the science of numbers has brought an ever increasing flow of inquiries for further information on this subject, revealing *You*—Whence? Why? Whither?

For those who seek to know *why* things are as they are and for the advanced student of numbers, this fifth edition is offered in the hope that it will stimulate still further his quest for knowledge and a better understanding of human nature.

In working with any principle new laws continually unfold. Hence, in the present edition we shall throw new rays of light upon your original portrait by numbers, sketched in the former editions. Chief among these are:

Your atomic structure, showing your electronic relation and reaction to the world in which you live.

Early history of numbers.

The law of the triangle and the square—a simple but necessary rule for success in all departments of life.

The application of the law of Algebra and English, "Two negatives make a positive," to name analysis.

List of Characteristic words which typify the meaning of each number in its 3-fold aspect.

Comparative analysis of two present day master types, Lindbergh and Byrd.

Other important additions are found throughout the book.

Our chief endeavor is to stress the most important point in all education—a recognition and understanding of the hidden power in each individual—his inner urge, that "unknown quantity," aside from heredity and environment, for which educators have so long been seeking.

HOW TO USE THIS BOOK

1. Write your Birth Name out in full.
2. Turn to page 38 and observe the Alphabetical Table.
3. Turn to page 41. Place the number value of Vowels above, Consonants below and Full Name on a separate line, as shown in David Wark Griffith. Add each name separately and then altogether. See Rule for Master Numbers, page 43, third paragraph.
4. Note the meaning of the Number Totals on pages 39, 40 and 53-67. If you are honest with yourself you can easily determine whether you are on the Positive or Reverse side of your vibration.
5. Turn to Chapter XV, p. 111. Apply the suggestions given to the first Vowel of first or last name, to the total Surname and total Signature and note the reaction.
6. Set out the Birth Date as shown in various examples in Chapter XXI, p. 142. Read again the meaning of the Numbers as suggested in Point 4 above and note whether you already have those qualities which you have come to gain.
7. Turn to Chapter XIV, p. 103, on Vocations and note whether or not you are in your right work.
8. Set out your most Frequent Signature. Read the meaning of the Totals as suggested in Point 4. Are they higher or lower than your original name? Have you grown?
9. Follow Outline for Analysis shown on page 84, treated in detail in Chapters IX, X and XI.
10. For adjustment of your Name to your birth path, follow suggestions shown in Chapter XIII, p. 95.

WHY STUDY NUMBERS WITH PYTHAGORAS?

The study of numbers is a study of the underlying law of the universe. Without numbers the world would be chaos, there would be no time and no dimensions of space. The statement of Pythagoras that "All is number" shows that as a "scientific genius of the first order" he anticipated the most scientific doctrine of our present age—"All natural phenomena may be expressed in mathematical formulae."

In the words of Lord Kelvin, one of the greatest modern physicists, "When you can measure what you are speaking about and express it in numbers, you know something about it, and when you cannot measure it, when you cannot express it in numbers, your knowledge is of a meagre and unsatisfactory kind. It may be the beginning of knowledge, but you have scarcely in your thought advanced to the stage of a science."

The reason that the science of numbers is just now receiving recognition is that it is only within the last twenty years that modern science has accepted the theory of Pythagoras and other Greek philosophers, that the world is built of atoms, vibrating at different rates of speed, and upon the varieties of these atoms, in number, size and aggregation, depend all the myriad forms of creation.

The atomic theory and other great truths relating to man and the cosmos were a part of the ancient wisdom, known chiefly to the priests, but through the succeeding periods of time preserved in large measure through the Masonic and other orders. In *The Pythagorean Proposition* by Elisha S. Loomis, the author states,

"A careful investigation of the great historic orders shows that each bore a striking similarity with modern Masonry as to tenets and rites; that each claimed esoteric wisdom and learning—the foundation on which Freemasonry of today rests.

"These facts and the additional fact that all learning and knowledge during these early centuries were in the keeping of the priests of the accepted religion of their times, and as these priests now controlled these scientific and secret orders, their only school of learning, making them the foundation of their religious institutions, it follows that Pythagoras, a leading metaphysician, mathematician and teacher of his day (569-470 B.C.) being highly educated in all Egyptian, Zoroastrian and Babylonian lore, must have been initiated into these secrets and mysteries, and that therefore he was an acknowledged and accepted Freemason as Freemasons were then known.

"Adorned with Virtue, Mercy and Justice, the three great attributes of Freemasonry, he became the founder of the Pythagorean school of philosophy, mathematics and religion, wherein arose the famous oppositions of philosophy, known as the ten antitheses of Pythagorean teaching, namely: 1. limited and unlimited; 2. even and odd; 3. one and many; 4. right and left; 5. male and female; 6. rest and motion; 7. straight and crooked; 8. light and darkness; 9. good and evil; 10. square and rectangle."

In *The Pythagorean Way of Life* by Watters, relative to the use made by Pythagoras of this law of opposites, it states, "The blend of the opposites produced a mean, or harmony, which he thought could be numerically determined just as that of the high and low notes of the octave had been. This theory of the blend he not only applied to music, but to medicine, to conduct, to everything in life."

A simple illustration of this truth may be seen in the fact that, "There could be no shadow if the sun were not shining." When shadows are removed, the brilliance of the light is dimmed. Attraction or good on every plane is the harmonious polarizing of the two opposing forces.

Pythagoras taught the unity of all things, that "Deity is the one, the Original Unity, the Infinite, out of which all finite things have come."

In his mind, philosophy, science and religion were one, the combined purpose of which was to bring man into union with the Divine. "By Philosophy he meant the quest of truth concerning man, nature, and God."

In Egypt he learned that, "The science of numbers and the art of will-power are the two keys of magic; they open up all the gates of the universe," and in his teachings he laid great stress on the discipline of the will into obedience.

"He discovered that the notes of the lyre were proportionate to the length of the strings, thus becoming the founder of the scientific theory of sound.

"He discovered the sphericity of the earth and was the first to recognize the slant of the zodiacal circle."

"He anticipated Copernicus by making the sun the center of the cosmos. In Geometry he enunciated and demonstrated the renowned theorem known to us as the 47th proposition of the first book of Euclid's *Elements* wherein we learn that:

" 'The square described upon the hypotenuse of a right-angled triangle is equal to the sum of the squares described upon the other two sides.' "

A close observation of this figure reveals that it has 12 sides, typical of the 12 signs of the zodiac, and the 12 types of people born in the 12 months of the year. It has 9 points of contact, where the lines converge—typifying the 9 paths of life which each individual must contact before he gains mastery on all planes, and thereby wins the right to direct wisely or counsel others.

"The ancients and Pythagoras himself, never meant to ascribe to numbers, that is to say, abstract signs, any special virtue," but as symbols of universal principles, they represent the chain of causation which leads back to the great Source of all and bring into greater harmony the three worlds, the natural, human and divine.

The Value of Numerology to You

The study of numbers gives you a knowledge of the *law* which governs your life. Being in the world, you are made of "world stuff" and are subject to like forms of measurement. Everything in the universe being of *One Substance, in different rates of vibration,* a knowledge of your own specific rate will enable you to attract success *now* instead of waiting for that big opportunity in the ever elusive future.

As a *wife,* it helps you to better understand friend husband and win his approval of your heart's desire.

As a *husband,* it enables you to be the real head of your own establishment and an acknowledged success in the business world.

As a *mother,* you will find it an invaluable aid in handling Margaret, William, Philip, Ann, or any child who has a decided mind of his own. It gives you a peep behind the scenes, into the child's own mind, and thus you have at once the key to the situation.

As a *teacher,* it will give you an understanding of each individual pupil and increase your success in a surprising manner, affording a most efficient method for the scientific study of human nature in all its varied aspects.

As a *young man,* it enables you to find your true vocation and thus save money and time in "arriving" at the top of the success ladder.

As a *young woman,* it not only gives you the opportunity to be popular, happy in your right work and attractive to the right man, but shows your ultimate purpose in life and the best methods for achieving your greatest ambition.

As a *salesman,* it provides you with a forehand knowledge of your customer and shows the proper stimuli to apply in order to obtain the desired reaction.

As a *business man,* it gives you a tip as to the best selling mediums and the most advantageous days for developing and promoting the various angles of your line.

As a *manufacturer,* putting a new article on the market, it enables you to attract success from the universal ether by use of the *right vibratory name,* thus assuring its appeal to the certain class of people whom you wish to reach.

As a *numerologist,* "Numerology Made Plain" affords you the most wonderful aid of any work in print. With over 1,500 indexed names, giving their vowel, consonant and total values, you have the largest store of information that has ever been compiled for this purpose. It will save you hours of time, and in addition thereto will enable you to give your client a choice in the selection of an efficient name. This in turn is bound to react to your benefit from every success standpoint.

As an *artist,* you have a list of over 1,500 names from which to select a winning nom de plume.

As a *writer,* the indexed list of names gives you scientific material from which to choose your characters, thus making them absolutely true to life.

As a *student of the occult,* this text gives you the answer to the eternal questions, "Whence, why and whither?" as well as to many things which have been a subject of wonder: "Why is A 1?" "How does my name affect me?"

"How do I attract my own happiness and success?" "How may I gain the help and protection of the universal forces?"

Whoever you are, whatever your problem, Numerology will help you to a better understanding of life. When you discover *why* things are as they are and *why* certain people react as they do, your perplexities will begin to dissolve and the sun will shine once more in your locality.

The most exact of all sciences in mathematics. The medium of thought is language. Based on the atom and electron theory, Numerology correlates the universal value of numbers with the rules of language and the law of vibration and gives to each individual a picture of his former self, his present status in life, and points the way to his highest goal.

If you desire to get the most out of life *now,* adjust yourself, through your name, to your own birth-path forces. Then all the universe vibrates with you and for you, work will be a pleasure and joy will attend each day.

Numerology is the most enjoyable route by which to gain a knowledge of the greatest law of the universe,— *vibration,*—which, when put into operation in your individual affairs, will bring order out of chaos and cause harmony, peace and happiness to reign supreme in your environment. It opens at once the door to *greater opportunity.* Seize it *now.*

The why of this science is a study in philosophy and metaphysics, but the universal meaning of the numbers never fails to be of absorbing interest to those who have learned their A, B, Cs. We trust that the pleasure and benefit derived from applying the rules in this new game of life will make you want to know more of the fascinating subject, portraying YOU—Past, Present and Future.

Numerology Made Plain

NOTE: *If you are in a hurry and have only a moment to spare, you will find the quickest method of analysis on page 119.*

CHAPTER I

YOUR NAME A WIRELESS PORTRAIT

DID you ever stop to think that your *name*, whether spoken (*sound* vibration) or written (a certain arrangement of letters, transferred to the brain by *color* vibration), immediately registers upon the mind of the receiver *a mental picture of yourself*, with all of your most prominent characteristics standing out in bold relief?

Your name broadcasts you to the universe. It gives an entire stranger thousands of miles away an insight into your subconscious mind, a knowledge of your talents, disposition and range of intellect.

Your name pictures you—all you *have been* and *are* at the present moment. It is your *trademark*, advertising to the world your own particular brand of success. Does it stand for efficiency as does the maid on Dutch Cleanser? Does it register 99 44/100 per cent pure worth like the soap "It floats"?

You are to the world what your name portrays. It leaves an indelible impression on your environment and associates, causing some to immediately like you (if they have harmonious vibrations) and others to avoid you. If you wish to know in what esteem you are held by acquaintances and friends, just figure out the various nicknames by which you have been labeled.

(15)

If *William* be your business signature, the one who receives your letter knows at once (if he knows the law of numbers) that you are a man with decided opinions of your own. You stand for principle, you finish what you undertake, you can be relied upon to keep your word, yet you have such an independent spirit that you do not take kindly to any suggestions from others. He will have to proceed tactfully and make you feel that *you* really know best how *this* deal should be handled. In *asking your advice* instead of advising you, he will strike a responsive chord which will arouse in you an interest in *his* proposition.

If *Bill* is your trademark, one can be more frank and open —your feelings are not so easily hurt. You are one of those "hail fellows well met," with physical magnetism and mental diplomacy, which make you an unusually splendid "driver." You can be depended upon to put the deal over though you have to fight for your rights every step of the way. You'll be just in your dealings, willing to meet the other fellow half way, yet he knows before he starts that his arguments must be sane and sound, practical and to the point, if he does not wish to return home with his armor punched full of holes. In the commercial world you're the "Big Boss," able to *"make it pay,"* and if you are really doing big things, and not too grasping for personal fame, the chances are you'll have more money than William or Will.

If your original name has shortened to *Will*, you are refined, cultured, artistic, hiding the stubborn streak of William under an outer garb of diplomacy. You have not the fighting qualities of Bill nor his keen sense of values, but you have infinitely more patience, a greater deference for public opinion, and much more style.

But if the fellows call you "Bill" and your wife says "Will," take it for granted that *she* considers you of much finer clay than do the boys with whom you travel. She may love you dearly, yet she will not "mind," and will be inclined to have things go her way. If you wish to be the "boss" yourself, train her to say *"Bill, dear"* (before she reads this paragraph).

Why the differences? Vibration.

Changing the spelling of your name makes you a different person because it changes your *rate of vibration.*

CHAPTER II

WHAT IS VIBRATION ?

YOUR breath is *one* vibration—inhaling and exhaling
—a positive movement with a reflex action.

The Century Dictionary says that vibration is "a movement to and fro," or "oscillation," as the forward and
backward swing of the pendulum of a clock.

Modern science says that *"all life is vibration,"* and
that without vibration there would be no life.

The first breath of life, when spirit entered matter,
set into motion or vibration universal forces of *creative*
energy.

You cannot limit the flow of energy in any form
without causing an entirely new aspect to arise. Stop
the flow of blood in any portion of the body,—congestion
immediately follows and causes a lump to appear. Build
a dam across a stream and you soon have a good-sized
reservoir.

Turn on the faucet and let the water run. The bowl
will soon be full, from whence the stream will continue
its course until it meets with an opposite force or certain
boundaries. When the space thus found has been filled
to the original water level a new outlet is sought, then
another and another.

The accompanying illustration will serve to show how
in like manner the great creative force, through the
medium of vibration, continues to activate larger and
larger spheres of activity.

Let the large circle represent the naught or chaos from
which the universe emerged. The first manifestation of

(18)

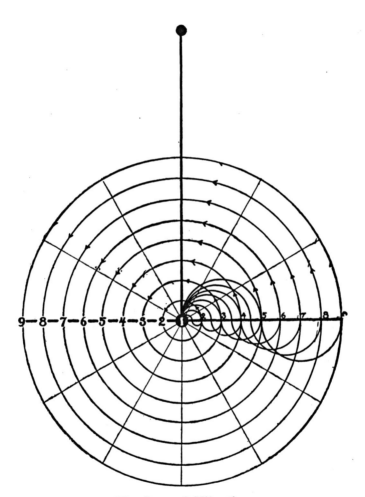

The Law of Vibration

life was the dot within the circle. While the earth is
not the center of *the* universe, it is the concentrated center
of our activities, and so we shall consider the dot in the
center of the accompanying sketch as the earth in its
primal form.

We shall not relate the various steps in evolution which
led up to Adam or the first man. These are found in the
first chapter of Genesis. We are concerned primarily
with Man from the time that he became imbued with
spirit and thus became a reflection of the Universal Intelligence.

The entry of spirit into matter caused a new influx
of creative energy to send its vibrations in all directions.
Just as a pebble thrown into the water starts a succession
of circular ripples around it, each individual wave going an
equal distance above and below the water level, so did the
first vibration or movement of spirit in matter cause everything to manifest a dual aspect.

In the human kingdom, the positive movement of this
first vibration is typified by Adam, the first man. As soon
as he arrived at perfection the negative or feminine
counterpart appeared in Eve, the first woman. With
the completion of this second unit of energy the great
creative force continued to pour its rhythmic current
through the dual aspect of the first vibration until a third
expression of life appeared. Now we have *father-mother-
child,* or *man, woman and the magnetic attraction between them—complete expression.*

Thus did life progress, each positive current of energy
being followed by its corresponding reverse aspect, these
two producing an ever higher expression, while the particular manifestations which characterized each successive

step became the symbols of the primary units of energy which produced them.

The Atomic Theory

One of our most modern interpretations of the universal law of vibration is found in the atomic theory. From our largest physical concept—the solar system—down to the smallest atom of which your body is composed, there is uniformity of design. The great law which guides the stars in their courses, rules in a like manner your entire existence.

Just as the earth revolves upon its axis, producing day and night, yet moves at a rapid rate of speed in its orbit about the sun, completing its cycle in one year's time, so does

The Law of Vibration represent a forward movement with a reflex action, moving in a cycle around a certain magnetic center.

Sir Oliver Lodge tells us that the atom "is a miniature planetary system with a nucleus of positive electricity surrounded by revolving negative particles or electrons."

Bertrand Russell in *The A B C of Atoms* gives a like picture and says that "the empty regions between the nucleus and the electrons fill vastly more space than do the units of the atom, so that the greater part of what appears to be a solid body is really unoccupied."

Thus we see that there is in reality no such thing as a true solid, only atoms moving in space.

Robert Millikan, famous scientist, describing the character of the atom, says "The number of negatives (electrons) held in the outer region varies from 1 in the case of hydrogen up to 92 in the case of uranium. The chemical properties of all atoms and most of the physical properties too, mass being the chief exception, are determined primarily by the number of these electrons which are found in the outermost shell."

Your Atomic Structure

In the great scheme of creation you stand between the atom and the solar system and partake of the nature of both. You are a unit of energy with a positive magnetic center, attracting into your world those people and experiences which are in some manner affinitized to your particular rate of vibration.

Your nucleus or motivating power is found in your date of birth. The individual digits of the month, day and year represent the ions or positively charged units of electricity in the nucleus of the atom, while the addition of these number values shows the force which is seeking to find expression—the inner urge which will color your entire existence.

As the number and arrangement of electrons in the atom characterize the element to which it belongs, so do the number and arrangement of the letters in your name indicate your character and quality of consciousness. They show the orbit in which you are moving or the sphere of influence in which you are most apt to be found.

As the atom in constant motion contacts other atoms and thereby loses some of its electrons or gains others, causing a different form to manifest, so are you influenced to a greater or less degree by contact with other individuals. This sometimes causes a definite change in name (as in marriage) or the forming of a business partnership. These close associations cause a readjustment of your personality and a different self may eventually manifest.

Each change of signature registers a new chapter in your life and indicates your present field of action.

CHAPTER III

YOUR RESPONSE TO THE UNIVERSAL KEY-BOARD

You as the highest form of creation on this planet include within yourself the primary elements of which this planet is composed. As iron, sulphur or gold each have certain properties, so do you possess certain dominant characteristics which correspond to the chemical element predominating in your system. Your reactions to life are largely in accord with the nature of such controlling factor, yet one should not forget that through the mind and the emotions, the chemistry of the body can be changed.

From the highest realm of thought to the densest form of matter, you have a definite point of contact with all planes of creation. Endowed with the power to think, you have under control, when you understand the laws that govern them, the lesser forms of energy.

Table of Energy Vibrations

The following table is compiled largely from a chart originally prepared by Sir William Crookes, famous English physicist and chemist, who discovered the metal thallium, devised the radiometer, and was one of the foremost experimental chemists of recent years, being knighted in recognition of his services to science.

Number of Vibrations per Second

Sound is the first form of energy above the plane of matter, its lowest and highest register upon the human ear being said to range from	16 to 32,768
Unknown	1,047,576
Electricity	$\left\{\begin{array}{l}33,554,432 \\ 1,073,741,824 \\ 34,359,738,368\end{array}\right.$
Unknown	$\left\{\begin{array}{l}1,099,511,627,776 \\ 35,184,372,088,832\end{array}\right.$

Heat	70,368,744,177,644 140,737,468,355,328 281,474,979,710,656

Light extends from heat, including infra
red, red, orange, yellow, green, blue, violet,
ultra violet to

Chemical rays	562,949,953,421,312 1,125,899,906,842,624
Unknown	36,028,797,018,963,268 72,057,594,037,927,936 144,115,188,075,855,872
X-Rays	288,230,376,151,711,744 2,305,843,009,213,693,952

The *Scientific American* adds

Gamma (radium) rays	480 Quintillion
Cosmic ray	720 Quintillion

Above these forms of energy which can be noted by our five senses, lies thought—the energy of mind—too rapid for measurement by physical means, yet more powerful in its effect than the average person realizes.

Your response to the various forms of energy indicates the measure in which you are attuned to life.

In the Realm of Sound—You are a Musician

Is your voice resonant with power and good-will? If you would have harmony in your affairs, guard well the waves of sound which go forth from your lips. All life is vibration and vibration is reflex action, within a cycle. Words sent forth into the ether bring back in visible form the manifestation of your spoken thought.

If you would know the effect that your words or your name can have upon you, observe the law of sound in music. Strains which have the 1-2-3 rhythm make one feel like dancing, those with 4-4 time stir a martial feeling, while others are but irritating noise to the cultivated ear, proving that

Sound, according to its rhythm, generates in individuals, corresponding feelings and impulses.

Whenever your name is spoken a certain sound vibration is put into the air which has a certain rhythm and a certain wave-length and generates in others within range, corresponding emotions.

When you change your name you change the rhythm of sound energy playing about you and different attributes begin to register.

Your Name also has its effect upon your outward appearance, due to the law of physics: "Sound creates form." Numerous experiments have been made in proof of this statement, such as sprinkling sand on a glass plate and drawing a violin bow across the edge. Each note will produce a certain geometrical design in the sand and when repeated will cause the same design to manifest again. "These invisible sound-vibrations have great power over concrete matter. They can both build and destroy. The human voice is also capable of producing these figures; always the same figure for the same tone." Thus does the spoken word bring into being crystallized thought-forms, geometrically produced according to the mental pattern held in mind.

Harmony in your Name

The vowels are the focal point of sound in any word, the consonants their setting. The vowels of your name reveal the inner emotional nature or soul which is seeking to come forth. The consonants of your full original name represent the body or form through which the soul is expressing, and give us an idea of your physical build and constitution. In your present name the consonants indicate your personality, your appearance and the impression you make upon others.

While the vowels and consonants together bespeak your hereditary talents and physical type, your most frequent signature represents you as you are, in your present environment. It shows your mental control, range of expression and whether you are playing on only one octave or the whole key-board of life.

If you would have harmony in your life, your key-board or range of expression (full name) should be in keeping with the music you have come to play—its dominant chord being found in your date of birth. In this the individual digits of month, day and year represent the primary motif, while the total of these three shows the keynote in which your varied life activities should be played.

These, in order to receive acclaim, must conform to the greatest medium for the enjoyment of music yet to be found—the radio. As any station can broadcast opera, speeches or baseball news at different periods of the day, so can you succeed in various lines at different periods of your life, provided that you, like the radio, operate on your own wave-length.

The specific wave of energy which governs the successful transmission of your message to the world, is found in your date of birth. With this your name should be in harmony if you would cause the world to listen and gain the best results from your own broadcasting.

In the Realm of Electricity—You are a Dynamo

The dictionary tells us that, "A dynamo is a machine for generating electric current by the conversion of motive power into electricity."

You would not attempt to use any electrical machine

without a knowledge of its purpose and how to turn on and off the current. You are the most intricate, finely adjusted electrical machine that ever was built. Do you know your own power, the work for which you are best adapted, and how to turn on and off the current—when to act and when to relax? The wise and proper use of the electrical energy flowing through you is what labels you a true success and gives you a paragraph in *Who's Who*.

A visit to any massage parlor reveals the fact that no two people can take the same amount of electrical current. This is one proof of our premise that you as an individual have a definite vibratory rate. When your normal rate can be determined, and your present rate, the difference between the two represents your problem. Raising or lowering it to normal offers the solution of the problem.

Your normal rate of vibration is found in your date of birth. This shows the amount of energy which is seeking to flow through you. Your name shows the type of machinery you are using and whether or not you are operating at full speed. It also indicates the character of your output or your present field of action.

Your name through its vowels (ideals and ambition), consonants (physical appearance and capacity) and final total (mental power) shows the manner in which you are handling the current or inner urge of your birth date.

Psycho-analysts tell us that the cause of all complexes is "failure of adaptation." When one's physical, mental and emotional machine is put in perfect order and properly adjusted to handle the current coming through, achievement is bound to follow.

In the Realm of Heat and Light you are a Radiating Center

As the sun gives light and heat to all, impartially, so are you the radiating center of your own world. Would you have recognition of your good qualities? Then you, like the sun, must continue to shine, 365 days in the year, at a seasonable temperature, refusing to scorch (with your tongue) or burn (with your temper) or allow the clouds to obscure the day.

No matter what appearances may be, you are the power center in your environment. If you raise your own vibrations to a higher point than those about you, the negative or destructive influences will have no power to retard your progress.

Can a chunk of ice affect a flow of steam? No, but the steam when brought to play upon the ice, causes it to dissolve, thereby raising it to the neutral point of water. If the steam continues to flow, the water is soon raised to its next higher form. Thus the lowest phase of energy has, by its opposite pole, been transmuted into increased power on the positive side. So can you turn your adversary into your own greater good through holding continuously the highest point of understanding in the matter, and radiating goodwill from center to circumference.

In the Realm of Color—You are an Artist

You have come with certain talents, materials and a picture to paint. The outline thereof is found in the month, day and year of your birth, while the colors with which you were originally supplied are found in your full original name.

With your first breath, the vibrations of the universe operative at that time, by involution, were registered upon your sensitive inner-self, more responsive than any photographic plate. These all your life, by evolution, are seeking to express outwardly.

As the artist with an order for a portrait begins with a goodly supply of colors, yet as he proceeds, discards some and adds others, so does your present signature indicate the shades which predominate and the progress you have made.

Your Intuitive Faculty an X-Ray

It has been found that a continued working with numbers —symbols of universal principles—causes the intuition to become more and more dependable. The meaning of each one of the nine numbers being reflected in everything identified by such number, a study of their symbolic attributes gives a new understanding of life. With a new point of view there comes an influx of new ideas. These in turn demand scientific proof of their authority, which when found, raise the standard and invite success on a higher level.

When the psychic force is trained to flow over a definite mathematical base its impressions become more reliable. Focus of the mental powers upon the problem of another causes the intuitive faculty to penetrate the consciousness of the other and bring the submerged impressions into the realm of visibility. When the cause is known, the remedy is more easily effected.

In the Realm of Thought—You are a Creator

Thought like other forms of energy, is governed by the laws which apply to all—two important rules being given by Edward F. Slosson, author of *Chats on Science*.

"All varieties of energy tend to run down from a higher and more concentrated form to a lower and more diffused form.

"Whenever there is a change in the form of energy, some of it becomes evenly diffused and unavailable."

This is why intense concentration on the matter at hand gives added power and speed in its accomplishment. The minute we hesitate or work in a lackadaisical manner our power is diffused and our energies scattered, and it takes us three times as long to accomplish the task.

Thought being a most powerful vibration, it can be invoked to handle your problem on the lower planes. As ice is crystallized water or the lowest manifestation of steam, so is matter crystallized thought. Would you have a joyous world? Proceed to use the law at your command. Speak your mental picture in clear tones, thus putting the pattern into the ether. Then welcome its return, but stand aside and do not impede its progress with your own opinions in the matter. Let the law work for you but leave the results to the Universal.

Think, speak, feel and act in the direction of your goal, discarding all deterrent factors, and you will soon know the joy of mastery through your own creative powers.

CHAPTER IV

WHERE DO THE NUMBERS GET THEIR MEANING?

Origin of the Digits and the Alphabet

The origins of language and mathematics are lost in antiquity, yet both can be traced to the same source—the endeavor of primitive man to further express his thoughts.

While tongues and alphabets vary, numbers have maintained a uniformity of design and a definite value throughout the world, showing that they are based upon certain universal principles. The particular meaning ascribed to each digit may be found by a study of the Hebrew Kabala, the sacred writing of the Chinese or the tenets of Masonry.

Not that numbers may be said to have any qualities or attributes inherent in themselves except as they acquire such through the association of ideas which accompany them. A $100 check is a symbol of that amount of money in the bank and may be of more value to you at the present moment than the money itself. Everything in life is in reality a symbol of some fact, idea or preceding cause, letters and numbers being our chief symbols for the expression of character and value.

The digits on which our system of numbers is based, are symbols of man's unfolding consciousness. The first spark of divinity which registered in man made him conscious of a vast world (0) in which he himself (1) was the chief actor and about which all else revolved. Applied to our own selves, 1 represents the ego, the individuality—the center of consciousness, the I Am—without which there would be none other. To our finite mind the universe can only be interpreted in terms of our own understanding.

Given a mate, man considered this to be an addition to

1 of 1 more—the second principle of combination, duality and the law of opposites.

Webster's International Dictionary gives the meaning of digit as "a finger or toe; one of the 10 figures or symbols— 0, 1, 2, 3, 4, 5, 6, 7, 8, 9—by which all numbers are expressed, so-called because of the use of the fingers in counting and computing."

While the fingers may have been man's first counters, he soon found that sticks could be used to present the same idea. Hence with the advent of the son, the additional unit used to express this idea brought into form the first enclosure of space—the triangle, symbol of the first completed family unit. This perfected father-mother-son principle was later transferred to man's highest concept of Deity, 1 symbolizing the Sun or father, 2 the Moon or mother, and 3 the Earth or son. This idea of the trinity is found in nearly all religions, from the earliest time down to the present day.

The 4 principle came into being when through the urge of necessity man had to parcel out a portion of land and till the ground. 4 rods would enclose a space sufficient for his abode. Thus 4 came to be associated with possessions, land, and those things which were definite and solid, which admitted of no argument and on which the primitive idea could stand.

Another aspect of the 4 is found in the shape of the figure itself. With its triangular top and vertical stem it represents the trinity or 3, plus 1 more, the projection of the completed unit into further territory.

In 4, man through his endeavor to subdue the 4 elements of earth, air, fire and water, found that certain results always followed certain causes. Thus in working with nature's

alphabet of color, sound, form and number, he developed a
conscious reasoning faculty through which he was able to
build his own ideas into definite form and complete his own
square of spirit, soul, mind and body.

While 1 always stands for the first principle, 2 for a
like or opposite force, 3 for the Trinity reflected in creation
as father-mother-son, 4 represents nature, the realm in which
humanity was placed in order to develop in 5, a true man,
conscious of the right use of his 5 senses, 5 fingers and 5 toes.

Here, with his arms and hands outstretched, man represents the 5 pointed star, conscious of all his creative powers
and yet who in his urge to use them, often burns his fingers.
Here he is given the freedom of will to observe, experience
and subdue the earth, yet he must be continually alert if
he wishes to maintain his dominion and not reverse his
powers.

The variable, versatile, magnetic, creative 5 is found not
only in the 5 symbols of Natutre's alphabet, the . 1 △ □ ○,
but in the 5 principal vowels of our own language, a, e, i, o, u
—the focal points of all expression.

In 6, man, having arrived at a state of conscious unfoldment, began to exercise selection in choice of a mate and
place of abode. Thus the cube or 6-sided figure represents
the home which man finally established for himself and
mate, while the hexagon reflects the same idea in nature
in the form of the bee's cell.

Six has always been associated with the idea of home,
marriage and domestic responsibility. It necessitates the
introduction of order and system into both mental and
physical activities. In Genesis we are told that on the
sixth day, man was created. Thus we have in this number
representing the highest manifestation of life on this planet,

the symbol of perfected physical and intellectual development.

Seven represents the introduction of spirit or completion —a sufficient relaxation from physical and mental effort to allow the intuitive faculty or spirit to come through. It represents the finished aspect of creation, 7 days of the week, 7 colors of the rainbow, 7 notes in the musical scale— the square (4) topped by the triangle (3), seeking illumination from above—God (3) and nature (4) combined in man.

Eight represents man having arrived at that point of intellectual attainment and spiritual perception where for the first time he gains mastery over his physical self and turns his creative force onto the higher planes.

In making the figure 8 the first stroke is the letter S, the serpent or the symbol of wisdom, the shape of the spinal column, through which the vital forces flow. When the S is crossed in the middle $ we have the symbol of the dollar sign. When one fixes his attention chiefly on the physical and commercial plane the lower portion of the 8 is closed and we may enjoy considerable success in a financial way.

It has been observed, however, that those who make the figure 8 in a reverse way (handwriting is a graph of the subconcious mind) have the sex problem to master.

By starting with the head of the serpent at the base of the brain and sending our mental force down to the Kundalini and up again at the base of the spine (the motion described in making an 8), we direct our energy in a constructive way—with the mind in control, but by starting from our emotions (or the end of the stroke) and ending at the head, we have allowed the lower self to control the higher.

Eight is always the symbol of evolution—the effort to establish a *balance*—of which our present 8 was originally the symbol. When one conserves his forces, he leaves no opening at either the bottom or top, but is at all times master of the situation.

Eight is the symbol of both death and regeneration and calls for mental alertness to direct and balance the situation. In the business world 8 is the large executive, who through mastery of his own forces is able to mould and handle others.

The eighth note on the musical scale completes the octave. It represents the 1 having arrived at the point of success and harmony. One and 8 are the only digits which represent the cube—the individual who has found himself, who knows how to conserve his energies and direct them into harmonious expression.

Nine is the trinity squared (3×3)—where man has reached that spiritual consciousness which gives him an interest in humanity far beyond the confines of his own personal or family interests. It is an urge to know and understand the law of life and is symbolic of the limit of conscious activity. The circle typifies the all inclusive, the circumference of every circle containing 360 degrees, the digits of which $3+6+0$ total 9.

Nine added to any number enables it to be reduced again to its original figure—9 plus 3 equals 12 and 1 plus 2 equals 3. It stands for expression in largest measure and yet in its opposite aspect is the principle of dissolution. It is indicative of action and reaction, yet represents the ultimate of all attainment—the greatest things in life to be desired.

Ten represents the total number of the digits and is considered the perfect number because it brings all things back to unity.   Here man has gained the consciousness of his one-ness with the Universal.   Through his contact with life in its 9 previous aspects he has gained the vision and understanding to start on a new spiral of achievement.   This is a turning point of great importance.   Here he must make a decision as to whether he will go forward into new and untried realms, leaving the old behind, or, fearful of the outcome, return and encounter the same experience again.

If he has learned his lessons well he will have no desire to repeat them but will gladly take his place among the leaders of men.   From 11 to 22, through mastery (see key

$$\frac{4112597}{29\text{-}11}$$

on page 40)   over each succeeding problem, he grows in knowledge, until in 22 he becomes a real master in his own world through a true understanding

$$\frac{411259}{22}$$

of the laws which govern.

The Numerals and the Alphabet

A, the first letter in most alphabets, is said to be traced to primitive man's experimentation with 3 sticks, which brought into being the triangle, or first enclosure of space. Subsequent forms likewise represented a unit of measurement and were later incorporated into the alphabet or language of such people.

"Our Arabic or more correctly, Indian digit characters, were derived from a form of Sanscrit, in which each of the first 9 numbers was expressed by a different letter of the alphabet; in that language the name of each of the first 9 numbers possessed a separate initial.   This useful system of writing numbers is of Indian invention."—Manley Hopkins: *The Cardinal Numbers.*

Among the early civilizations the Hebrews, Aryans and Greeks used numbers in place of letters, giving to numbers a specific significance. The 22 letters of the Hebrew alphabet were used for numbering in the order in which they stood, the first 10 representing the digits, the following letters expressing 20, 30, etc. and then 100's.

Letters, being mathematically evolved, *are* numbers. Both are symbols, letters giving us the quality, numbers the value, of that which lies back of the outer form.

It is interesting to note that the Old Testament was written in Hebrew, with an alphabet of 22 letters. The New Testament, Matthew excepted, was written in Greek, with an alphabet of 24 letters. The wide spread circulation of the Bible has been due to its translation into English, with an alphabet of 26 letters. Reducing 26 to 8 gives the number of evolution, but adding to this the & sign, which is considered correct by some authorities, we have 27 or 9— the limit of computation on this planet.

CHAPTER V

VIBRATION APPLIED TO THE ALPHABET

ATTACHING numbers to the 26 letters of the alphabet in the order of sequence, we find that eventually each one comes under the influence of one of the nine digits:

A	B	C	D	E	F	G	H	I
1	2	3	4	5	6	7	8	9

J	K	L	M	N	O	P	Q	R
10	11	12	13	14	15	16	17	18
1	2	3	4	5	6	7	8	9

S	T	U	V	W	X	Y	Z
19	20	21	22	23	24	25	26
1∅	2	3	4	5	6	7	8

Why is A 1?

Right here you have a right to ask, as have the most intelligent men the writer has known: "Admitting the truth of what you say as to our particular characteristics, how do you arrive at such conclusions? Why is A 1?"

The letters of our alphabet have stood in their particular order of succession for hundreds of years and have long since absorbed the universal characteristics which are transmitted by the respective digits to all things having their particular number value or rate of vibration.

Other Alphabets

"Granting even that, how does this vibratory law apply to other languages, when the alphabet is not the same and the letters stand in a different order?"

The law of vibration is universal in its application. Anything which a number or digit determines will take on the aspects of that vibration when it has been under such

(38)

influence for a long enough period of time to have absorbed such qualities into its nature.

The law applies to each alphabet as it stands, the difference in word values showing a fine distinction in the
way different nationalities have grown to regard the same
thing. Take for example the letters of the Hebrew alphabet, which in the order of sequence stood for certain
steps in the evolution of the Cosmos as do the nine digits.
Do you think for one moment that the ancient Hebrew,
if transplanted here, would view any one thing in our
modern existence in the same light as the average man of
today?

Hence, taking into consideration the time element, a
new vibration or change of name will not affect an individual immediately unless his or her inner self has
grown to meet it. They must wear it long enough to
absorb the universal vibrations behind it before it really
becomes a part of their nature.

How the Digits Influence Our Alphabet

The twenty-six letters of our alphabet, having stood in
their present numerical order for centuries, have absorbed
the qualities of their controlling digits,—

1 transmitting its particular aspect of universal intelligence to the letters A, J, S, giving them *creative*
powers, with *initiative, daring, independence* and the *pioneer spirit.*

2 giving to B, K, T *diplomacy* and *tact*, with *imitative*
and *collective* qualities.

3 causing C, L, U to find *joyous expression* in *art* or
humanitarian lines.

4 endowing D, M, V with a good *intellect*, a *con-*

scientious sense of duty and enjoyment of life in *work or study.*

5 bringing many *changes* to E, N, W, making them *"go-getters"* for *experience—versatile, active* and *charming.*

6 making F, O, X the best *mothers, teachers* and *human benefactors.*

7 throwing *spiritual* qualities over G, P, Y, with a desire for *perfection, wisdom and authority.*

8 bringing *money* to H, Q, Z when they direct their energies wisely and unselfishly, with justice and tact.

9 giving I and R success in *art, literature* and the *healing* profession, with the entire world for their field of expression.

In addition to the nine digits we have two master numbers,—11 and 22,—which throw leadership qualities around the other numbers to which they are related.

11 stands for a *new beginning* in a higher cycle, a greater spiritual unfoldment, with *inspirational* and *psychic* qualities.

22 is considered the highest vibration of all, being represented in the universe by the Trinity, 3, the 7 planets and the 12 signs of the zodiac. 3 plus 7 plus 12 is 22. 22 links the spiritual with the material and *makes inspirational things practical, directing large enterprises with diplomacy and tact.*

Numbers Applied to the Name

Take the name David Wark Griffith, one of our most famous moving picture producers, and attach the number value of each letter (using the table shown on the first page of this chapter).

Place the digits representing the vowels above, the con-

sonants below, and the full name on a separate line, adding the digits of each name separately and then altogether.

```
                11          +     9   = (11-9)—Soul-talents
             10          1       18
Vowels:      1 9                 9  9
             DAVID   WARK   GRIFFITH
Consonants: 4  4  4    5   92   7 9 6 6  2 8
             12         16        38
              3          7        11
                  10                   = (1-11)—Body—
                                            personality
Full name:  4 1 4 9 4  5 1 9 2  7 9 9 6 6 9 2 8
                  17            56
              22        8         11      = (22-8-11)—Intel-
                                            lect and destiny.
```

All double numbers are reduced to single numbers by
the addition of their digits with the exception of 11 and
22, the master vibrations. These always stand out by
themselves, expressing their leadership qualities through
the smaller numbers to which they are related.

The above name is an unusual example of the far-reaching influence of an individual who has master numbers in
every position—vowels, consonants and full name.

The *vowels* of your full name reveal your *natural talents*
—those things in which you have previously scored success,
and which are now stored within the realm of your *subconscious* mind.

The *vowel* digits of 11-9 which are shown above, indicate
that Mr. Griffith in a previous lifetime was undoubtedly a
promoter and leader (11), a pioneer (1) and inventive
genius (1) in the field of art or humanitarian (9) endeavor.
This would give him a natural ambition to excel in such
lines now and to think in world (9) terms.

Your *consonants* represent the physical body through which your mind in expressing. They reveal your *personality*—the impression you make upon others.

The above *consonant* vibration of (1-11) shows that Mr. Griffith is a dynamic, enthusiastic individual who cares naught for precedent or what other folks may think. The 3 of David shows his appreciation of the beautiful and artistic; the 7 of Wark, his eye for detail, perfection and finish, while the 11 of Griffith immediately stamps him as a leader in any field, interested in something "different," something large, yet having an inspirational or uplifting effect.

Your *full name* shows the intellectual growth you have made in previous lifetimes and indicates the *destiny* which you have now come to fulfill.

The above name has two master numbers in the individual name totals; so we do not add the 3 names together and obtain a final total, as is usually the case.

The total digits of (22-8-11) indicate that Mr. Griffith came to earth this time endowed with a most powerful intellect with which to work out a destiny of universal magnitude. The 22 shows ability to *analyze* and *organize* the inspirational ideas of the 11 vibration and carry them out in an *executive, forceful, money-making, successful* (8) manner.

The leadership qualities of 11 and 22 make this individual an unusual *business* (8) *engineer* (8) in the line of dramatic art, where the imitative qualities of 8 combine with the innate *artistic expression* of 9. Mr. Griffith must work with a *big, immense idea* to be a genuine success, for his are universal vibrations. A limited environment or sphere of action would cause his own strong forces to revert disastrously upon him. "To whom much is given, from him shall much be required." Mr. Griffith's unparralleled success shows that *fortune* and *fame* await those who have the courage to live up to the demands of their own high vibrations.

Two Rules to Remember in Name Analysis
Always hold 10 a 10 and do not reduce it to 1.

The writer's experience in analyzing thousands of names has proven beyond any question of a doubt that 10 should always be held intact and not reduced to 1. This makes a great difference in many cases.

When the vibrations of given names add up to 11 or 22, this indicates possibility of leadership in such directions, hence in the vowels of David Wark Griffith the 10 of David added to the 1 of Wark makes the total vowel (11-9).

The cipher can of course be crossed off for the purpose of shortening your addition, after notice has been made of the possible total, as is indicated in the consonants of the above name. It should be held, however, when by doing so an 11 or 22 is obtained.

High Numbers—10-11-22—should always be considered in their lesser aspect.

In Mr. Griffith's full name, the 22-8-11 total, reduced, would be 4-8-2, adding up to 14 or 5. This gives him versatility and adaptability in throwing his leadership qualities over a wide range of activity. It should make him a master (22) of c h a r a c t e r, in which line he has truly

$$\frac{381913259}{41\text{-}5}$$

achieved his success (8).

CHAPTER VI

THE STORY OF THE NUMBERS

EACH letter of your name, by reason of its numerical position in the alphabet, has a certain rate of vibration. Each vibration has certain characteristics. Therefore, you as an individual are a composite of all the qualities which the letters of your name symbolize, the highest number in your name indicating your present stage of growth or development.

This is not your first appearance on the earth planet. You have been here before, each time with a new lesson to learn. The various stages through which you have passed are revealed by the

22 Steps in the Success Ladder

0. The *cipher* or naught stands for the period of chaos before time began. It also symbolizes the boundless space from which all things came forth. The first manifestation of life was the dot within the circle, "representing the sun in the center of the zodiac, the giver of light, life and energy to its system. . . . Every unit of life is the center or dot of its own universe, has its own sphere of activity and influence, and rate of vibration." (Key to the Universe, Curtiss, pp. 57, 59.)

1. The *first* manifestation of motion in the Cosmos, or spirit coming down into matter, is symbolized by the straight line. It represents the primal cause and stands for the principle of unity in all things. "1 cannot be divided; multiplied by itself it still maintains its unity, yet it creates all others." Thus we have *creative ability, daring* and the *pioneer spirit* symbolized by the digit 1.

2. The first vibration, generated by the contact of spirit with matter, is typified in its positive aspect by Adam, the first man, followed by Eve, his feminine or negative counterpart, gaining her way by artful diplomacy. Thus we have two units of energy representing the complete expression of the first vibration, giving to the digit 2 the qualities of *duality, diplomacy* and a *receptive, feminine nature.*

3. The great creative force working through the two aspects of the first vibration produced a third unit of expression. Thus 3 marks the completion of the first earthtrinity, *father-mother-child,* and stands for *complete and joyous expression on the nature plane.*

4. Having attained physical perfection, man found that after all he was not quite satisfied. He looked about and began to wonder why. He started to reason things out for himself and thus evolved his intellect. He found that lasting good only came to him when he himself was "on the square." Proof of one principle gave him a burning desire for more until we find him early and late striving to make more money with which to further pursue the path of intellectual attainment. A true 4 is always *busy, energetic* and *on the square,* ever seeking more *proof* and greater *knowledge.*

5. Arrived at a stage of mental supremacy, the individual longed to try his powers. In doing so he met with many varied experiences and some bitter lessons until he made the big discovery which restored to him his balance. He found that knowledge alone was not sufficient to bring his heart's desire and that only when absolute master of self and all his physical passions could he dominate others through his own magnetic powers. *To know life* *from every angle with unbounded freedom* of thought and action is the constant desire of 5.

6. Having, like the prodigal son, traveled in a far country and drunk his fill, the 5 individual decides to return home and settle down. He comes to the conclusion that life after all is what we make it and every responsibility has its corresponding reward. Domestic life "looks good" to him; so he establishes a home and raises a family, which develops his backbone. He becomes a prime factor in the promotion of *education, health* and *human betterment* in his community, deriving a keen enjoyment from the free advice he gives to others. The sterling qualities gained here are found in *mothers, teachers, doctors, welfare workers* and all others who stand as *guardians of the home, school and society,* in whose names the 6 vibration is usually strong.

7. Having worked hard to rear his family, educate them and fit them to take their place in society, the 7 individual feels that he is entitled to a *rest* from manual labor. He seeks out a *quiet place in nature* and sits down to think things over. After all, is there not something more to be attained? He knows the road that he has come; he has left no details undone to reach his present state of *perfection.* He is sure of himself in this respect and resents any suggestions from others. Yet his *intuition* tells him that there surely must be some higher laws than those of the purely material world, which laws, if put into operation in daily affairs, would bring results much quicker. He acts on his hunch and begins to study the *occult* and *metaphysical* laws on which he formerly looked with disfavor. He sees at once that *the higher law must always include the lesser* and begins to figure out

how things can be done without so much mental and physical effort. Wonderful ideas present themselves to his inner searching mind. Here is the wisdom for which he has been searching, which he now must tell to all mankind. Hence we find many *preachers, teachers* and *religious* and *metaphysical writers* predominating in the 7 vibration.

8. Having gathered a store of mystical lore with which to enhance his fortunes, the 7 individual is asked by many who hear him so eloquently expound, "Have you proved these principles out for yourself? Do you know by experience just what they are worth?" 8, being an honest soul, with good fighting qualities and a keen sense of justice, determines to show his materially-minded friends the concrete proof of what he preaches, so he enters again the commercial world and puts his theories into practice. They stand the test, and he finds that rest after all was not what he wanted. He goes to work with added zeal to make his declarations real and finds that a *perfect balance* of wisdom and work, love and justice, ideas and materials, plus an *intelligent driving force,* brings money, success and fame by a much shorter route than his purely laborious reasoning efforts. Thus 8 becomes the "big business" man, the *large executive,* tempering reason with intuition, justice with love and force with diplomacy.

9. Increased material success having come through the use of the higher laws in the material world, the individual realizes that even with money and fame he is not entirely happy. He notes the trouble and lack, so totally unnecessary, in the lives of those about him, and develops a sympathetic interest in their welfare. His *positive efforts to help the other fellow* to a higher understanding of life attract a reflex current of thankfulness and good-

will, bringing in their wake more wealth and a greater enjoyment of life than when he worked in the 8 vibration. The *inspiration* which comes to the 9 who truly *loves* his fellowman enables him to express his *splendid artistic talents* in a more *universal* way. Opportunity for extended *travel* comes to him, with attendant growth and renown. Famous *singers, artists* and *world travelers* are generally strong in the number 9.

10. Having passed through the varied experiences of the 9 vibrations, man stops to survey the road he has traveled. He is a wiser man than when he started. With a knowledge of all his past joys and sorrows stored within his subconscious mind he now stands ready and strong to proceed on his way, but before he can enter a larger field he has certain tests to pass. He must prove he has learned his lessons well, and that through his knowledge of the higher laws he can create out of his own aura, if need be, all things needful for his supply. Here his friends may think him queer, he may meet with loss and adversity, in order to test his mettle, yet he must firmly stand his ground. As 10 has a wealth of inner wisdom, he must take the advice of none save the still small voice within if he desires to enter a higher cycle and enjoy success that is real and lasting.

11. Having stood the tests of *aloneness, adversity* and *financial stress* which often beset the 10 vibration, and having come out on top, man is allowed to make a *new beginning* in a larger field of activity. Here his subconscious mind, stored with the knowledge of all the past, enables him to speak and act inspirationally. He immediately knows how a thing should be done, though he may not be able to tell you why. This is the reason that

a boy or girl with an 11 vibration in the name generally has trouble with the teacher. He thinks he knows best. His soul has grown to the point of mastery and he will not accept commands from others. He can only be reached by persuasion and an appeal to his own superior self. It is important, indeed, that he be well grounded in education and the higher laws of life, else disaster will follow in his path by reason of his strong force going in the wrong direction. An 11 is a dynamic individual, with *enthusiasm, inspiration and ideas,* which he *must give out to others* if he desires a reflex of good himself.

12. Having made a new beginning in a higher cycle, the individual passes through the next or twelfth grade in school. Here he has the triangle of complete expression represented 4 times (4×3). He has gained mastery on all planes, the digits of the number itself forming the complete triangle of 1-2-3 (12 is 1 plus 2, which equals 3). In 3 man attained physical perfection; in 8, physical and mental; in 9, physical, mental and emotional; in 11, physical, mental, emotional and spiritual, while 12 includes them all, being the number of numerical completion shown by the 12 months of the year, the 12 signs of the zodiac, etc.

13-20. From this point man goes by successive stages through the lessons of the 13, 14, 15, 16, 17 and 18, similar in nature to those of the first nine vibrations, yet with greater creative force and a farther-reaching influence. At 19 he has another testing period before being allowed to start on the first round of the third and higher cycle, signified by 20.

21. In 1 and 2 we had the masculine and feminine in their individual aspects; in 12 we found man and woman working together, with man directing the activities of the opposite sex, but in 21, the beginning of the third cycle of evolution, we find conditions reversed, and the woman in the lead. The individual has now gained perfection in three worlds (21 is 3×7), physical, mental and spiritual, and is called upon to exercise his powers. When a man reaches the age of 21 he is considered an individual of discretion, capable of using the ballot wisely.

22. Twenty-two represents the illumined intellect, where man, through the use of his perfected powers, becomes absolute master of his own environment. 22 equals 2 plus 2, or 4. 4 has the knowledge of 1, 2 and 3 plus his own additional wisdom. Hence 4 equals 1 plus 2 plus 3 plus 4, which is 10, or the foundation of a never-ending spiral of manifestation. Having grown wise through suffering, man has learned to know and obey the higher laws, by which he makes his dreams come true and his inspirational ideas develop into practical realities. He has learned how to co-operate intelligently. While in 21 the feminine aspect was in the lead, in 22 we have the perfect balance of man and woman and their joint creations, each allowing to the other perfect freedom of thought and action.

$$\begin{array}{c c c c c c} \text{M} & \text{A} & \text{S} & \text{T} & \text{E} & \text{R} \\ 4 & 1 & 1 & 2 & 5 & 9 \\ \hline & & 22 & & & \end{array}$$

Until man is master of himself and his environment he cannot be truly a wise counselor to others. Those who have come to earth with a master number (11 or 22) in their name have been through all of the first nine grades. They are here now to shed their light on souls less developed than themselves. A real 22 is often found in diplomatic circles or as a humanitarian adviser of the highest order, where his inspiration and psychic qualities, combined with his understanding, tact and executive ability, make him a leader to be reckoned with in any situation.

22 gains success through knowing the law, putting it into operation and then passing such knowledge on. When he has gained mastery over all things here he undoubtedly will find new worlds to conquer.

Warning to the High Numbers

If you have an 8, 9, 11 or 22 in the digits of your name or birth date you have passed through the 7 vibration, where you reached the peak of accomplishment for self alone. You must now work for the good of many and enlarge your interests to take in the whole world. You have developed a strong and powerful force, which must be used in an equally large manner. No matter how conscientious you may be, if you confine your activities to your own family circle or small group of associates, you are inviting disaster upon yourself. It is like trying to put 22 pounds of steam pressure into a boiler built for only 7. An explosion is bound to occur. The high numbers are meant to help the lower and bring them up to their own high plane of understanding. When they do not act in this capacity, they dig their own graves and conduct their own funerals.

Life is growth, and growth is ever upward and outward. We must keep on going. There is no such thing as standing still. The law of vibration is the law of opposites. If we do not go forward we are pushed out of the way to make room for someone else. "If we refuse to take a firm stand on the positive side of good, we are swept into the opposite current." (Curtiss.)

CHAPTER VII
THREEFOLD MEANING OF THE DIGITS

WE have found that the law of vibration is the law of opposites. We can swing as far in one direction as in the other. The stronger our force, the greater our power for good or ill. Midway between the two extremes there is a point of negativity where the individual may be called "lukewarm"—he is neither hot nor cold. Such a person becomes the prey of the more positive minds about him and attracts trouble and loss through his own inertia.

The universal meaning of the numbers in their positive, reverse and negative aspects is given below. In the Cycle of Nature we have the triangle of 1-2-3; in the Cycle of Man, the square of 4-5-6-7, and in the Cycle of Superman, the reflection of the 1-2-3 principle 4 times in the triangles of 10-8-9, 11-8-9, 10-22-9, 11-22-9.

THE CYCLE OF NATURE: 1-2-3
The Digit 1

POSITIVE—*Creative ability*, originality, individuality, intuition, concentration, aspiration, independence, aggressiveness, initiative, strong intellect, and a daring pioneer spirit, with *unity of thought and action* characterizing all activities. Inventors, pioneers, promoters are found in the 1 vibration.

1 is a part of every number and hence exerts a strong influence over all other vibrations. Should a name be made up of the digits 3-1, as in Mary (3) Pickford (1), it would show *creative* ability in the field of art and self-expression (3); if it were made up of the digits 4-1, it would indicate originality in mechanical design or a builder of efficiency systems.

REVERSE—A reverse 1 is arrogant, domineering, egotistical, inconsiderate, selfish, self-centered, determined upon own satisfaction, irrespective of others.

NEGATIVE—A negative 1 is dependent, weak, lazy, submissive, mentally asleep, limited in thought, action and expression.

The Digit 2

POSITIVE—*Duality*. Even in its positive aspect 2 stands for duality. It can exercise the strong qualities of 1 and be alert and aggressive or operate through the more sociable, diplomatic and feminine side of its nature. It is co-operative, kind, a collector and builder—an excellent compiler of statistics, data and information for others to handle.

REVERSE—Critical, nagging, fault-finding, always worrying about what other people may think, posing for effect, susceptible to flattery, selfish, unreliable, too proud for own good.

NEGATIVE—Indifferent, careless, no pride in personal appearance, unsociable, unable to make up his mind on anything and stick to it, so negative and impressionable that he becomes the tool of stronger minds about him.

The Digit 3

POSITIVE—*Complete and joyous expression in art or humanitarian lines*—a child of nature. 3 is master on the material plane, combining the creative ability of 1 with the building and collective powers of 2 into a happy expression of those things which make for *comfort, health and pleasure.* He knows how to promote his own personal ambitions through the initiative of 1 and the tact of 2, excelling in music, art, literature, law, nursing and the healing profession, or in any avenue which calls for *self-expression* in

service to others.   We find many 3s associated with tea
rooms, beauty parlors, millinery and gift shops.   Their
sense of humor and agility in repartee make them popular
as toastmasters and after-dinner speakers.

REVERSE—Selfish, sensual, debased, scattering forces,
living alone, impatient, important, egotistical.

NEGATIVE—Repressed, unsociable, unreliable, careless in
dress, unresponsive to music or art, dependent, lazy and indifferent.

THE CYCLE OF MAN: 4-5-6-7

The Digit 4

POSITIVE—*Builders on material and intellectual planes,*
conscientious, "on the square," always busy, mentally and
physically.   4 makes a splendid bookkeeper or mechanic;
he is mathematical, methodical, analytical, reasoning, honest, a master of detail and routine.   He is a splendid builder of systems for greater economy, efficiency or output.
His ambitions are of a personal nature, for his own self-
development, yet of all employes he is the most conscientious and faithful.

REVERSE—Critical, self-limited, a drudge and hard
worker, with his nose to the grindstone, so economical that
he makes the eagle scream, so analytical that he refuses to
listen to his hunch but reasons himself out of his good intentions.

NEGATIVE—Despondent, buried beneath adverse circumstances, financial limitations and hard work, a plodder
without any desire for intellectual development.

The Digit 5

POSITIVE—*"Go-getters" for experience—investigators of
life from every angle.*   5 is a lover of freedom, change,

variety, new scenes and new contacts, versatile, magnetic, charming, a good mixer, a splendid judge of human nature, interested in philosophical and metaphysical research, a good character analyst. 5 is strongly sexed, yet master of himself and able to quickly adjust himself to any environment. He is a rejuvenator and enthusiasm-generator on all planes —the traveling salesman, the vaudeville player, the "noted lecturer on psychology."

REVERSE—Dominated by sex, here today and gone tomorrow, always looking for greener pastures, absolutely unreliable, the destroyer of homes, peace and pleasure for selfish gratification, interested in black magic.

NEGATIVE—Physical, mental and financial failures, living a life of monotony and hardship, the result of their own self-indulgence and instability.

The Digit 6

POSITIVE—*Guardians of the home, school and society, assuming responsibility graciously.* A 6 is a natural mother, a splendid teacher, or a good business man, always interested in the welfare of others, although he clings closely to his own family circle. He is energetic, absolutely reliable, a good money-maker, a splendid talker—if he does not talk too much. Many literary and professional people, especially in healing lines, are found in this vibration.

REVERSE—One of those who will argue "until the cows come home" without being able to get the other fellow's point of view; anxious, worried, self-centered, so wrapped up in "his own" that he does not care to bother with others. His obstinacy causes others to leave him alone, and, being one of those individuals who simply must talk with someone, he becomes blue and depressed. He feels that others do not appreciate his efforts to share their responsibilities. When he learns to stay in his own yard he will be a much happier individual.

NEGATIVE—Overburdened with too many cares; the "goat" for the rest of the family, the office force, or unappreciative friends; lacking in self-esteem, indifferent as to his personal appearance.

The Digit 7

POSITIVE—*"Reservoirs of wisdom"* who have to be "pumped" before you really discover their depth. 7 stands for perfection, finish, culture, poise, self-confidence, attention to detail, and a firm, positive will. 7 is sensitive and proud, inclined to hold himself somewhat aloof from the common crowd, hiding his hurt feelings beneath an outer cloak of cold indifference. He can be generous, gracious and affable; at other times he desires to be left strictly alone, to meditate undisturbed. He is a lover of nature, intuitive, psychic, interested in the mystical and occult. He keeps his own counsel and the confidence of others, yet because of his secretive disposition is often lonesome and misunderstood. He must learn to say what he thinks and "get it off his chest" if he wishes to live in a happy environment. A 7 should work in an individual capacity where he is absolute authority in his own realm. He can do well in the professions, in real estate, agriculture or the religious and metaphysical world.

REVERSE—Domineering, dictatorial, restless, roving, leaving things undone, failing to keep appointments, stubborn, opinionated, atheistic, satirical, with no appreciation of the finer things of life and no leniency nor sympathy for the other fellow's views.

NEGATIVE—Lacking in self-confidence, unable to express what he feels, a mystery to himself, misunderstood by others, too introspective, afraid to put his best foot forward, a dreamer instead of a doer.

THE CYCLE OF SUPERMAN: 8-9-10-11-22
The Digit 8

POSITIVE—*A balancer of spiritual and material things,* the big business man, who puts inspirational ideas into concrete, or any other *building* material which he may be using. An 8 is the large executive who uses tact, diplomacy, co-operation, keen discrimination and an intelligent driving force to bring his business, art or commercial affairs to a *successful* conclusion. He is an engineer of large projects, an investor of funds for others, a leader in financial circles, a wielder of power and influence.

REVERSE—One who uses his social position, power or money for selfish purposes, a merciless driver, money-mad, supercritical, unappreciative, unaccommodating, unfeeling, inviting his own ruin and disaster.

NEGATIVE—Unlucky, apparent victim of circumstance, unsuccessful in business, investments or social ventures, due mainly to his own selfish nature. An 8 has reached the plane of superman, where he must think of others as well as himself. Until he acts constructively for the good of all he will continue to meet with adversity.

The Digit 9

POSITIVE—*Lovers of all humanity, expressing in a large way their splendid artistic talents.* Both money and love

Money and Love

46557	3645
27	18
9	9

come to the 9 who sets into operation a positive current of good-will, sympathy and helpfulness toward everyone he meets. He has a strong emotional nature, broad sympathies and an intelligent understanding of others' needs and wants. He should not be satisfied with mediocre success; the *world* is his field of expression. Many inspirational writers, artists, healers, humanitarian workers and world travelers are found in the 9 vibration.

REVERSE—Selfish, miserly, sarcastic, critical, arousing destructive passions in others, "trying to get something for nothing by playing on another's sympathy, fear or unsuspecting mental attitude."

NEGATIVE—One who gives everything away, whose heart rules his head, too sympathetic for own good, used by others to further their ends.

The Number 10

POSITIVE—Same as 1, with the addition of *authority, completeness* and a larger viewpoint. The lessons learned in his transit through the 9 vibrations have given the individual a greater understanding of life, more sympathy with the shortcomings of others and more confidence in his own creative powers. A person whose name totals 10 can get the viewpoint of anyone with whom he may be talking *if* he makes his own mind receptive at the time.

REVERSE—Same as reverse 1—arrogant, covetous, gratifier of selfish ambition, irrespective of cost to others.

NEGATIVE—Dependent, lazy, one who starves in the midst of plenty.

The Number 11

POSITIVE—*Inspiration. Enthusiastic, dynamic promoter of the higher truths.* An 11 in the name indicates that the individual is an *old soul,* one who has come to illumine the way for others less developed. The wealth of wisdom stored within his subconscious mind makes him psychic, sensitive to atmosphere, environment and personalities, full of original ideas which must be given out if he does not wish his own strong force to revert disastrously upon him. An 11 should work with the public in a large way, as a lecturer, writer, teacher, preacher or promoter.

REVERSE—Debauched, miserly, degraded. Promoters of diabolical schemes and nefarious practices.

NEGATIVE—Lacking in self-esteem, no faith in anything, unaware of their own powers, or so spiritually minded and impractical that they are forced to rely upon others for their financial support.

The Number 22

POSITIVE—*A master on all planes—making inspirational things practical.* One who by use of the higher laws has become absolute master of his own environment and is thereby fitted to give wise counsel to others. Great executives, diplomats, corporation heads, statesmen and promoters of humanitarian projects on a large scale are examples of the progressive 22, while bookkeepers, clerks and office managers who abound in this vibration are those who are not aware of their large potential powers.

REVERSE—Promoters of get-rich-quick schemes, big talkers and small doers, deceitful, vain, proud, archcriminals.

NEGATIVE—Lazy and selfish, allowing their own strong force to revert to a 4, which puts them in a limited environment, forced to take orders from others when they should be holding the reins themselves.

CHAPTER VIII

Words whose Number Values Prove the 3-fold Meaning of each Vibration

Using the key on page 38, each word has the total value of the number under which it is shown.

The reverse and negative characteristics are put into the same group for the purpose of greater ease in comparison with the positive aspects of each number.

10

I d e a
9 4 5 1

———

19

—

10

Positive	*Reverse or Negative*
Ambitious	Timid, lazy
Fortitude	Unfaithful
Heaven	Hell
Idealistic	Dreamer
Integrity	Deceit
Initiative	Retiring, cautious
Liberty	Problems
Intelligent	Materialist
Adam, air, ahead	Poor, Common

Emotion, man, number
Numerology, perfect, pioneer
Primary, spirit, union, united
Variety, writing, young

2
B a l a n c e
2 1 3 1 5 3 5
—————————
2Q

Alert		Death, Delay
Analyst		Crank
Kind	•	Cross
Steady		Jealous
Cork		Decay

Music, Noah, occult
Will, Caesar, rule, show

3
A r t   F a m i l y
1 9 2   6 1 4 9 3 7
————   ————
 12   30
————   ————
  3   3

Friendly	Critical
Good Nature	Sarcastic
Humanitarian	Radical
Humor, Happy	Fear
Observing	Egotistical
Romantic	Hysterical
Sell	Sex
Sociable	Swear

Daughter, son, doctor
Absorb, actor, charity
Electricity, entertainer
Lawyer, marry, nursing
Promoter, responsibility, writer
Edison, Will Rogers

4
F i g u r e s
6 9 7 3 9 5 1
40

Busy	Anxious, Evasion
Conscientious	Gambler
Defense	Aversion
Design	Destruction
Endurance	Self-Pity
Neat	Old
Patient, politics	Opposition
Sensible	Stingy
Originality	Curiosity
Judgment	Spendthrift
Bookkeeper, accountant	Materialistic
Fiction, mathematics	Work (22 reduced)

5

L i f e   E x p e r i e n c e
3 9 6 5   5 6 7 5 9 9 5 5 3 5
23—5   59—14—5

Generous	Odd
Investigate	Shrewd, Corruption
Interesting	Emotional
Intuition	Impulse
Power	Impatience
Swift	Cruel
Manager	Sensitive
Character	Temper
Easy	Affected

Aim, aspire, automobile
King, Christ, Roosevelt
When, where

6	
M a s o n r y	E d u c a t o r
4 1 1 6 5 9 7	5 4 3 3 1 2 6 9
33	33
6	6

Adviser	Bold
Active	Hesitant
Ability	Abrupt
Affectionate	Sentimental
Athletic	Crude
Benevolent	Selfish, War
Cheerful	Cross-grained
Confidence	Conceited
Dramatic	Visionary
Knowledge	Self
Order	Adversity
Psychologist	Nervous
Truth	Conceit
Banker, broker, cafe	
Costumer, detail, druggist	
Drugs, hotel, manufacturer	
Musical, secretary, teacher	

7	
S c i e n t i f i c	T e n a c i t y
1 3 9 5 5 2 9 6 9 3	2 5 5 1 3 9 2 7
52	34
7	7

Courage	Discouraged
Domestic	Extravagant
Idealist	Egotism
Industrious	Pride
Refined	Curious
Religious	Sensuous

Serious   Secretive
Will-Power   Cold, abusive
Silent
Investments

Control, dancing, finisher
Earth, farmer, finance, nature
Financier, honesty, mother
Orderly, plan, real estate, stage
Speculative, political, Coolidge, Ford
Psycho-analyst

$$
\begin{array}{c c}
 & 8 \\
\text{S u c c e s s} & \text{B u i l d e r} \\
1\ 3\ 3\ 3\ 5\ 1\ 1 & 2\ 3\ 9\ 3\ 4\ 5\ 9 \\
\hline
17 & 35 \\
\hline
8 & 8
\end{array}
$$

Action   Doubt
Analytical   Critic
Ardent, Influence   Crooked
Co-operate   Deceive
Courageous   Cupidity
Diplomacy   Impatient
Game   Grudge
Philosophical   Deceptive
Religion   Flattery

Engineering, examine, happiness, values
Independence, intellectual, legacy
Memory, responsible, sense, spiritual
Tenacious, trained, unity

$$\begin{array}{ccc}
& & 9 \\
\text{L o v e} & \text{L a w} & \text{E x p r e s s i o n} \\
3\ 6\ 4\ 5 & 3\ 1\ 5 & 5\ 6\ 7\ 9\ 5\ 1\ 1\ 9\ 6\ 5 \\
\overline{18} & & \overline{54} \\
\overline{9} & 9 & \overline{9}
\end{array}$$

Artistic	Vulgar
Big	Conservative
Business, Leader	Failure, lack
Confident	Quiet
Love	Anger
Money	Economical
Inspiration	Plodding
Publicity	Exaggeration
Service	Selfishness

Literary, cashier, corporation
Dance, designer, health
Newspaper, sun, world, leader

$$\begin{array}{ccc}
& 11 & \\
\text{M a s t e r y} & \text{E n e r g y} & \text{L i g h t} \\
4\ 1\ 1\ 2\ 5\ 9\ 7 & 5\ 5\ 5\ 9\ 7\ 7 & 3\ 9\ 7\ 8\ 2 \\
\overline{29} & \overline{38} & \overline{29} \\
\overline{11} & \overline{11} & \overline{11}
\end{array}$$

Able	Plodder
Abundance	Loss
Adventurer	Practical
Advertising	Indifferent
Clever	Simple
Creative	Negative
Emotions	Calm
Fire	Destructive
Independent	Dual

White   ·   Black
Wisdom   Caution
Generosity, pleasing, preacher
Psychic, radio, speedy, winner
Youthful, numbers

$$22$$

M a s t e r	M i n d	W o r k
4 1 1 2 5 9	4 9 5 4	5 6 9 2
22	22	22

Capable   Aloof
Food   Dope
Self-Esteem   Possess
Statesman   Liar
Speed   Gamble
Talker   Clerk
Lord, water

One of the best ways to determine whether the individual is functioning upon the positive or reverse side of his vibration is to obtain a page of his handwriting in ink, on unruled paper.

The handwriting is an unconscious portrayal of the subconscious mind and shows at a glance whether the individual is optimistic or pessimistic, hesitant or aggressive, generous or economical, intellectual or emotional, stubborn or diplomatic. Many texts can be had on this subject, hence we are merely calling attention to this means of proving your findings through numbers.

CHAPTER IX

YOUR NAME REVEALS YOUR PAST

ENLARGED family portraits on the parlor wall are now a dim recollection to most of us, but if you would like a glimpse of your former self, set out your name and view yourself through numbers.

Your *original full name,* impressed by your soul upon the minds of those about you at the time you came to earth, registers your stage of growth and development in previous lifetimes. It is a picture of You from the past, revealing your latent powers and true nature.

Setting out the original name of a prominent world figure, we have:

```
         6      +      7      +      3      = 16=(7) - Soul —
                      16            21                talents.
Vowels:  6         1  9 6      6   5 5  5
         J O H N   D A V I S O N   R O C K E F E L L E R
Conso-   1   8 5   4  4 1  5    9 3 2 6 33 9
nants:       14         14            35
             5          5             8      = 18=(9)—Body—
Full                                              personality.
name:    1 6 8 5   4 1 4 9 1 6 5   9 6 3 5 6 5 3 3 5 9
           2 0         3 0            5 6
            2          3              1 1
                    5                        = (5-11)-Mind—
                                                  destiny
```

11 being a master number, we do not reduce it to 2 but add the remaining digits, making the total 5-11.

Soul—Natural Talents (Vowels)

The *vowels* of your *original full name* reveal your *natural talents.* They represent your soul or subconscious mind, in which is stored the record of your past achieve-

(68)

ments, giving a natural desire to repeat your success in such lines now.

The *vowels* in the above name, 6-7-3, which total 16 and then 7, indicate that in a previous lifetime Mr. Rockefeller was undoubtedly a lover of nature (7), active in the field of finance (7).

The 6, which is also the first vowel, indicating the domestic "type," shows that he had learned to assume responsibility graciously, that he could talk (6) or keep silent (7). The 3 tells us that he was an ambitious soul, with an appreciation of the beautiful in all things and a saving sense of humor. The 7 total shows self-confidence, a firm, positive will and the determination to see everything through to the finish. His love of nature (7), still evident in Mr. Rockefeller's fondness for golf, developed a keen intuition, an inner religious nature and a desire for supreme authority in his own particular realm.

Body—Personality (Consonants)

The *consonants* of your *original name* represent your *body*—the materialized form of all your previous thinking. They reveal your *personality* or the impression you make upon others.

The *consonants* in the above name are 5-5-8, which total 18 or 9. 5 and 8 are two of the strongest physical numbers, indicating that Mr. Rockefeller was endowed with a good physical constitution. The two 5's made him a good judge of human nature, amiable and adaptable, the 8 gave him diplomacy, tact and driving force, while the 9 bestowed a strong and pleasing personality, able to *attract* those things which he desired.

Mind (Full Name)

Your *original full name* shows the *intellect* with which you came.

The 2 of John indicates that Mr. Rockefeller had learned how to collect ideas, materials and people and handle them in a systematic, tactful manner. The 3 of Davison shows ability to give complete expression to his own idea without any outside assistance.

The 11 surname shows Mr. Rockefeller to be an *old soul*, one who has previously achieved mastery of certain spiritual truths and who has come now to act in a larger, more universal capacity.

The total name vibration shows through the 5 that Mr. Rockefeller is a born investigator, interested in life from every angle, a splendid judge of human nature. These qualities coupled with the dynamic 11 make him a master salesman and promoter of new and advanced ideas, able to sell his products or schemes, whatever they may be, with agility and speed. The 11 gives him many inspirational ideas, far in advance of the present moment, and endows him with that psychic sense or bird's-eye view which "gets him there" ahead of time.

CHAPTER X

YOUR PRESENT PHOTOGRAPH

YOU ARE what your name signifies. The world accepts you at your *name value*, your *usual signature* being a complete picture of yourself at the present moment.

Notwithstanding your youth and inexperience, you are older, more enduring and a far greater achievement than the Egyptian pyramids, the greatest example of perfection in the material world. Perfection of any kind is shown by a reflection of the trinity (triangle) in some form. In the pyramid, built on a square foundation, with its sides made up of 4 equilateral triangles joined at the top, we have the trinity reflected 4 times.

You, like the pyramids, are built on a square—*soul* (vowels), *body* (consonants), *mind* (full name) and *spirit* (birth path), while the triangles or trinities of numbers present in your name (1-2-3, 1-5-7, 2-4-8, 3-6-9, 8-9-10, 8-9-11, 9-10-22, 9-11-22) register your achievement in complete expression on the various planes.

As the pyramids with their 4 triangles (4×3), the 12 months of the year and the 12 signs of the zodiac all represent numerical completion, so there are 12 points by which we gauge your intelligence, bearing and inner nature.

1. Your Type (First Vowel)

The *first vowel* of your name, *modified by any preceding consonants, reveals* your *type*. It is the pivotal center of your subconscious mind, indicating your dominant reaction toward life.

Using the signature by which Mr. Rockefeller has been known for many years, we have:

$$\frac{6}{} \quad + \quad \frac{3}{\overline{21}} \quad =(9)\text{—Soul—subconscious desire.}$$

Vowels: 6   6   5   5   5
        JOHN D. ROCKEFELLER
Consonants: 1 8 5   4   9 32 6   33 9
        $\frac{14}{}$ $\frac{35}{}$
        $\overline{5}$ + 4 + $\overline{8}$ =17 (8)—Body—personality.

Full name: 1 6 8 5   4   9 6 3 2 5 6 5 3 3 5 9
        $\frac{20}{}$ $\frac{56}{}$
        $\overline{2}$ 4 $\overline{11}$ Intellect and
            6   =(6-11) present plane
                                of action.

The *first vowel* in the above name is "o" (6), modified
by the preceding consonant "J" (1). Thus Mr. Rockefeller would be interested in those things which pertain to
business, home, education and human betterment (6), but
he would want to carry out his activities in such lines in
his own individual (1) way.

2. Subconscious Desire (Total Vowels)

The *vowels of your present signature reveal your subconscious desires.*

Mr. Rockefeller has in the vowels of his present name
the trinity of *complete expression,* 6-3-9, showing that in
whatever field he chose to function he would be able to put
his ideas over in a convincing manner. The 6 gives him
a love of home, business and educational projects, the 3 a
desire for individual self-expression, the 9 an interest in
world affairs.

It is interesting to note that the medium through which
Mr. Rockefeller achieved wealth and fame is made up of
the same vibrations as the *vowels* of his name:

$$
\begin{array}{ll}
\begin{array}{ccc}
6 & 9 & \\
O & I & L \\
& & 3
\end{array} & \quad -15=(6) \\[4pt]
& \qquad\quad -(3) \\[6pt]
\begin{array}{ccc}
6 & 9 & 3 \\
\hline
& 18 & \\
\hline
& 9 &
\end{array} & \qquad\quad -(9)
\end{array}
$$

Mr. Rockefeller found in oil the very thing which he desired and which his subconscious mind knew just how to handle. This may account in some measure for his phenomenal success and for the money which followed.

$$
\begin{array}{ccccc}
M & o & n & e & y \\
4 & 6 & 5 & 5 & 7 \\
\hline
& & 27 & & \\
\hline
& & 9 & &
\end{array}
$$

3. Personality (Consonants)

Your *consonants reveal your personality,* the impression you make upon others.

The *consonants* in the above name are 5-4-8. The 5 makes for geniality, an investigative nature, love of variety and new experiences. 4 exercises a somewhat counter influence, setting into operation a strong current of economy, thrift, practicality, proof and a conscientious performance of duty. The total of 8 shows a strong personality, executive ability, tact and an intelligent driving power with which to carry his ideas to a successful conclusion.

4. "Stock in Trade" (Surname)

Just as one man starting in business would handle hardware, another merchandise and another be a promoter of plays, so does your *surname denote the materials with which you came.*

The 11 of Rockefeller shows a universal, big idea, and

the necessity of dealing with the public in a large way. As a capitalist Mr. Rockefeller is working in his own vibra-tion.

```
C  a  p  i  t  a  l  i  s  t
3  1  7  9  2  1  3  9  1  2
              38
              11
```

5. "Modus Operandi" (Given Names or Initials)

Your *given name, or the initials which you are using, show the manner in which you are handling the "ma-terials" of your surname.*

The 2 of John shows system (2) in the collection (2) of ideas (11), materials, statistics and information from all corners of the earth with which to build (4) a more efficient, economical and mechanically perfect system of big business. The 4 enables him to detect the leaks, to be observant of the necessary detail, to live, work and give in a regular manner, exercising keen discrimination, good judgment and reasoning qualities.

2 plus 4 is 6, indicating that he will use his inspirational ideas (11) in business, home and educational avenues.

6. Present Plane of Action (Signature Total)

Your *total signature shows your intellect and present plane of action.*

6 is usually a conservative business man, but when we link it with the dynamic 11 we have truly a master mind, who will project inspiration and enthusiasm into business, educational and human betterment lines, attracting a re-flex of new and larger ideas, to be again sent forth to all mankind.

While Mr. Rockefeller's fame is linked with oil, which has the same vibrations as the vowels of his name, he put

himself in still greater harmony with the universal forces
by operating under the name of the

$$
\begin{array}{ccc}
\text{S T A N D A R D} & \text{O I L} & \text{C O M P A N Y} \\
\text{1 2 1 5 4 1 9 4} & \text{6 9 3} & \text{3 6 4 7 1 5 7} \\
\hline
27 & 18 & 33 \\
\hline
9 & 9 & 6
\end{array}
$$

$$\frac{27}{9} + \frac{18}{9} + \frac{33}{6} = 24 = (6).$$

His business name carried the same total vibration as
his own signature (6-11). Through promoting (11) a
medium of the same vibration as his vowels under a business name vibrating the same as his own signature, he came
"into his own" as a capitalist (11).

7. Planes of Expression (Nature—Man—Superman)

The three planes of expression on which man functions
at the present time are: Nature (1-2-3) or the physical,
Man (4-5-6-7) or the mental, and Superman (8-9-10-
11-22) or the spiritual.

To find on what plane the individual is most active, set
out the digits in their order and place under each one the
number of times such digit occurs in the name, using an x
to indicate the individual or full name totals.

We are showing the letter values of Mr. Rockefeller's
name below. The complete chart at the beginning of this
chapter will give you the individual and full name totals.

$$
\begin{array}{l}
\text{JOHN D. ROCKEFELLER} \\
\text{1 6 8 5 4   9 6 3 2 5 6 5 3 3 5 9}
\end{array}
$$

x =Totals		Nature			Man			Superman			
	1	2	3	4	5	6	7	8	9	11	22
Vowel "			x		x			x			
Cons. "	1	1	3	1x	4x	3		1xx	2		
Name "		x		x		x			xx		
		5			8			5			
		xx			xxxxx			xxxxx			1+6=(7) keynote

=16 letters

We find that Mr. Rockefeller is active on all three

planes, with an even number of total digits on the planes of Man and Superman. This shows a well balanced individual, able to make his inspirational ideas practical.

8. Keynote (Number of Letters in Name)

Your *keynote* or present groove of thinking *is shown by the number of letters in your name.*

There are 16 letters in the above name, showing Mr. Rockefeller's interest in finance (7) and his strong love of nature (7).

9. Temperament (Odd or Even Numbers)

"A predominance of *odd* digits shows an emotional, inspirational nature which rebels at discipline and routine. Such a soul wants plenty of room to carry out its own ideas in its own way and finds joy in self-expression through art or humanitarian lines.

"*Even* digits show a practical, reasoning, methodical, constructive, executive mind, able to build, imitate and polish the creative ideas of the odd digits and make their dreams concrete realities." ("The Science of Numerology"—Author.)

1 is considered neither odd nor even.

In the above name there are 6 even numbers, 9 odd, and one 1.

While Mr. Rockefeller has more *odd* digits than even, there are a sufficient number of the latter to give him a good balance and to allow his spiritual qualities of inspiration and intuition to take the lead. His original name being 5-11, both odd numbers, and his original vowel vibration 7, also odd, it is important for him to have a predominance of odd digits in his name; otherwise his cold reasoning faculties would kill his inspirations and good intentions.

10. Dominant Traits (Predominating Digits)

Your predominating digits show characteristics of corresponding nature, while the total absence of any vibration indicates that such qualities should be developed.

If you have many more 5's in your name than any other number you are of an investigative nature, a lover of travel and variety, a good judge of human nature, interested in psychology, metaphysics and the occult, ever searching for more knowledge and a new experience.

Mr. Rockefeller has four 5's in his name, showing his breadth of view and his keen zest in life, which will keep him forever young. The three 3's, three 6's and two 9's all show wonderful ability in the expression of his big idea, with interest in health, education, domestic and world affairs.

11. Complete Individual Expression (Trinities)

Complete individual expression, or the ability to carry out your own ideas without assistance from others, is shown by the trinities in your name.

In order to put over any project successfully you must have the *creative ability* and *aggressiveness* of 1, the power of *collection* of 2,—whether it be of materials or people, —and the ability to *express your idea in complete form,* the attribute of the 3 vibration. If you are lacking in one of these three primary elements of success you will be forced to call upon someone else to supply the missing link.

If you are going into business for yourself you should have one of the following trinities present in the total digits of your name:

1-2-3 (create, collect, express)—Balanced expression on the material plane in those things which make for health, comfort, pleasure, beauty and self-satisfaction. (On the higher planes 1 is found in 10 and 11, 2 in 4-6-8-22, 3 in 6 and 9.)

10-8-9, 11-8-9, 10-22-9, 11-22-9—Balanced expression on the high plane, assuring success with the public in any line harmonious with your birth path.

Other trinities which will give you power along certain lines are:

1-5-7 (start, investigate, finish)—*Science and philosophy*. These numbers show strong intuitive faculties and interest in scientific, philosophical and metaphysical research. They are character analysts, philosophers, teachers, preachers and scientists.

2-4-6-8 (collect, build, maintain, operate)—*Business, manufacturing, engineering and dramatic art*. These give intellectual and analytical qualities with strong materialistic tendencies.

3-6-9—*Creative expression in art, literature or humanitarian fields*. These show a strong emotional nature, with enthusiasm and inspiration characterizing their efforts.

In the chart of Mr. Rockefeller's name shown at the beginning of this chapter we find a vowel total of 9, a consonant of 8, with 11 in the full name, giving a trinity of complete individual expression on the plane of Superman. The 11 shows a mind full of inspirational ideas, the 8 a strong personality with which to build them into form, while the 9 gives an inner understanding of just how to express his idea in the most complete, artistic manner. Such a trinity is a guaranty of large success to anyone who conscientiously lives up to such vibrations.

Noting the particular lines in which his powers will be most apt to find expression, we find in the individual and full name totals the complete *business* trinity of 2-4-6-8, while the vowels show a third—3-6-9, complete expression in art, education and humanitarian avenues.

Three trinities!—complete expression on three planes —a wonderful name, which cannot possibly escape success if the individual plays up to his own forces.

12. Self-Esteem and Balance

The vowels in your name indicate your self-esteem, your real self-value. This does not mean egotism, but the true gauge of your inner powers.

If your vowels and consonants are the *same* in value, there is a perfect balance between your inner and outer self. You are what you appear to be.

If your vowels are *lower* than your consonants, you have personality,—you enjoy helping others but take a back seat yourself. Build up your self-esteem and your health will improve accordingly.

If your vowels are *higher* than your consonants, you have the knowledge. Build up your personality and make people like you.

The vowels in Mr. Rockefeller's name total 9, his consonants 8, a strong number on the same plane. The 9 shows plenty of self-esteem, yet we know that it will temper his sense of justice (8) with sympathy and kindliness.

The total of 6-11 throws all of his final digits—vowels, consonants and full name—on the high plane, showing a powerful name, able to express his ideas in a universal, masterful manner.

Comparing Mr. Rockefeller's present signature with his original name we find that he is a much bigger man than when he came. His original vowel vibration of 7 has been raised to 9, showing a growth from individual ambition to interest in world affairs. His original name totaled 5-11, his present signature is 6-11, showing that he has become more stable, more dependable, that he has developed more interest in human affairs, and now stands like the rock of Gibraltar, impervious to the winds of fate or the tide of public opinion.

CHAPTER XI

SQUARE YOUR DESTINY WITH YOUR BIRTH PATH URGE

T HE *destiny* which you have come to fulfill *is shown by the total digit of your original full name.*
To reach this goal successfully you must learn the lesson of your birth path and incorporate the spirit of its vibration into all of your activities. Your life picture is not complete without the square of soul, body, mind and spirit, or your past, present and ultimate goal, revealed in the total digits of name and birth date.

Your name reveals your trinity of soul (vowels), body (consonants), mind (full name), but in your birth date we find the spirit or fourth dimension which you have come to gain.

The famous geometrical theorem of Pythagoras—"The square of the hypotenuse of any right-angled triangle is equal to the sum of the square of the other two sides"—is an apt illustration of every life. It not only represents the 12 types of people in their 9 points of contact with the world but in its 3 squares, the 3 periods of endeavor which must be met and mastered by each one during his journey here.

In dealing with any problem we would be entirely in the dark if we did not know the nature of the question. Hence in the problem facing you we do not look for its solution through heredity or environment alone but go to the crux of the matter, the peak of the triangle, the starting point for You on this planet—your *date of birth*—which registered upon your inner self in definite outline the *urge* which brought you here.

Your first mark in this world or *the vertical line of your right-angled triangle, is found in the digit of your month* which governs from 1 to 27 years of age.

This shows the character of training or the preparation which you should have received for your life work during this time. Since "well begun" is half done, if your early years were in accord with the constructive influence of your month, you should have squared the vertical line of your triangle—in the *morning* of your life and be able to handle well the larger tasks of your day.

The base line of your triangle is found in the digit of your day, which governs from 27 to 54 years of age.

Here you put your education and training into practice and if your energies are thrown into lines of activity harmonious with your day vibration, you should enjoy happiness and financial success. Through concentration on the work in hand you can *square your base line* to such an extent that by the age of 54, when you come under the beneficent influence of your year, you can take the afternoon off if you desire.

No building is true unless the corners are square and the proper angle established. The angle of your month and day is a specific influence throughout your life. *Your dominant vibration for every year is found by adding the digits of your month and day to the current year.* Thus it will always color your activities. Its vibrations must not only be met separately, during their respective periods, but together as well, if you would have harmony in your affairs.

The hypotenuse of your right-angled triangle is found in the digit of your year, governing from 54 to 81 years of age.

Your Year represents the afternoon of your day, in which you can work or play, according to your personal interest in the matter. It indicates the "finished" aspect of your work or its avenue of service. Squared, through perfection in quality and wide range of usefulness, it gives you the joy of "arrival" and the satisfaction which can only come from work well done. It not only brings the answer to your problem but gives you a chance to prove whether your previous efforts have been wisely spent. If your own life is a "good example" for other souls to follow, you should radiate your light to all who cross your path,—and be generous with your counsel—when asked.

Morning (month), mid-day (day), afternoon (year) and evening (total birth path) represent the four periods of your present cycle of existence. If you start right, with your plans well laid, if you keep your mind on your work during the main part of the day, you should in the late afternoon, have time for a round of golf and enjoy the society of friends in the evening.

The nature of the group with whom you associate at this time will depend largely upon your achievements of the day. If you continue to be a "live wire," with a keen interest in life, you have a long period, from 81 to 108, to enjoy the fruits of your labors amid the glories and beauties of earth. But, if you have "played" when you should have been working, and have allowed the erroneous impression of "age" to register upon your soul, the chances are that after the age of 81 you will return to your second childhood (the digit of your month) and go to bed early, under the dictation of others, instead of enjoying the fullness of life under the vibration of your total birth path.

Outline for Analysis

Using the 47th problem of Euclid as a method for solving your own problem, we have the following points for consideration in the order shown:

THREE ANGLES TO YOUR LIFE PROBLEM
I—THE INNER URGE
Found in the Total Birth Date

1. The spirit which must be instilled into all of your activities and your medium of achievement (total birth path digit).
2. Method, point of contact, preparation and training (digit of month).
3. Specific character of your work (digit of your day).
4. Finished aspect of your work and its avenue of public expression (digit of your year).

II—YOUR DESTINY
Found in Full Original Name

5. Goal of achievement and intellectual capacity (full original name).
6. Hereditary traits, shown by surname, modified by individualistic expression of given names.
7. Subconscious, soul, or emotional self—your natural talents and lines in which you would be most apt to excel as a child (vowels of full original name).
8. Your physical constitution and personal appearance (consonants of full original name).

III—PRESENT ENVIRONMENT
Found in your most frequent signature

9. Present field of action and mental control (total of most frequent signature).
10. Self-esteem and ideals (vowels).

11. Personality and influence (consonants).

    a. The relation of consonants to vowels and total name shows whether or not you are easily influenced.

    b. Trinities in the name show balance—lack of them, certain qualities missing.

    c. Is total name or outlet, large enough to handle the vowel and consonant vibration?

    d. Is the name positive, reverse or negative in its aspect?

    e. Are there any digits entirely missing?

12. Harmony of Name with Birth Path.

    a. Is total name as high or higher than birth path?

    b. Are vowels in harmony with birth path total?

    c. Is name total in harmony with birth angle of month and day (month and day added together)?

Brief Sketch of Name and Birth Date

Using Mr. Rockefeller's name and birth date as an example, we find in searching for his inner urge that he was born

$$\text{July 8,} \quad \frac{1839}{21}$$

7 8 $\overline{3}$—18—(9)—Spirit or inner urge

In writing an analysis we would not list the points as shown here, but would make it a more personal story. Until one is familiar however, with all the important steps to be considered, it is well to write them down in the order shown.   They must all be analyzed before any correct deductions can be made.

I—THE INNER URGE

1. The spirit which Mr. Rockefeller must instill into his activities is a large one—based on the 9, the symbol of

world (9) service (9) and good will. 9 stands for the
ultimate or the all inclusive circle of 360 degrees (3 plus 6
is 9). Expression from center to circumference is imperative
if a 9 $\dfrac{5679511965}{54-9}$ wishes to enjoy happiness at his own
center. Because a 9 extends farther, and because it includes
all that have gone before, a 9 can do himself more harm
than anyone else can do. Should he indulge in criticism
or a self-centered attitude, he pulls the world in upon himself and becomes cramped for want of room. Health (9),
love (9) and money (9) are the portion of the 9 who ren-
ders a big (9) service (9) to the world (9).

Success always comes easier when one works in his own
vibration. In oil (9) Mr. Rockefeller used a medium
which brought him the money (9) which made him famed
throughout the world (9).

2. The 7 vibration of his month gave Mr. Rockefeller
a strong contact with nature (7) and earth (7). Oil
comes from the ground and in the handling thereof he
gained recognition in the field of finance (7). As a finisher
(7) of each task as it came to hand he exercised the will-
power (7) and stick-to-it-iveness which makes for *quality*
service. A 7 should be the "last word" in whatever he
undertakes and should put a scientific (7) background of
technique under his efforts. In building up an unusual
organization, outstanding for its *standard* of service, he
made the vertical line of his own birth path the pivotal
key-note of his business success.

3. *The base line* of Mr. Rockefeller's success (day of 8)
might be said to lie in his unusual capacity for business
organization. Through the Standard Oil Company and its
many subsidiary corporations he has enjoyed the reflex of

financial reward rightfully due the strong executive (8)
who is capable of engineering (8) his plans through to a
success(8)ful conclusion.

4. The *hypotenuse or finished aspect* of Mr. Rockefeller's work (year of 3)—its avenue of expression, from
the standpoint of *Oil*—may be found in the joy it brings
to the automobile and pleasure loving world.

From the standpoint of money alone, Mr. Rockefeller
is making humanity (3) happy (3) through his various
bequests to philanthropic and educational projects.

As a financier (7) and builder (8) Mr. Rockefeller has
maintained the angle of his month and day throughout his
activities. 7 plus 8 is 15 or 6, in which capacity as an
organizer (6) he has brought his many big (9) ideas into
concrete realization.

Very active during his month and day, he has been able
to take a large part of the afternoon off for several rounds
of golf, and to help others get a greater enjoyment out of
life through his contributions to their welfare. Now in the
evening of his stay, in the conscious use of all his faculties,
he comes into the fullness of his cycle, into a realization and
appreciation of the law (9) which brings all things to pass.
He can enjoy life as never before—he has learned the
secret,—that a continual new idea, put into action every
day, is the mystic way to the fountain of youth.

II DESTINY and HEREDITY

5. Mr. Rockefeller's destiny as shown by the chart on
page 68 is 5-11 or 7 in its lesser aspect, standing for power
(5) and mastery (11) in the field of finance (7). The
complete scientific trinity of 11-5-7 gave him a keen searching mind, able to handle large problems in unusual ways.

6. From the standpoint of heredity, his surname of 11 gave him intuitive, psychic (11) power, able to promote advanced ideas before the public and yet maintain a deep respect for and interest in spiritual things.

The 2 of John endowed him with patience in detail and ability to absorb, handle and build system (20) into his work, while the 3 of Davison gave him a sense of humor (3) and an interest in happiness on the physical side of life.

7. His original 7 vowel gave him not only a love of nature but will-power and stick-to-it-iveness, and an instinctive interest in financial problems.

8. His consonants of 5-5-8 totalling 18 or 9 showed a virile, youth-renewing constitution, with good recuperative powers, able to attract both people and things through the power of his own magnetism.

He had every number in his name from 1 to 11, hence a point of contact with all types of people—an important factor in the success of any public man.

III—PRESENT ENVIRONMENT

9. Mr. Rockefeller's most frequent signature, John D. Rockefeller, shown on page 72, higher in its total of 6-11 than his original name of 5-11, shows development and growth. As an organizer (6) it gives him mastery (11) in the realm of business, education or humanitarian projects. In its lesser aspect of 8 it shows financial success through the large constructive service of 6-11, the extension of his activities through many channels.

10. The present vowel of 9 not only shows the self-esteem he should have, commensurate with the work he came to do,—found in his birth path of 9, but it contains

the complete trinity of expression, 6-3-9, giving him a desire to express in world (9) wide lines.

11. The 8 consonant shows a strong executive personality. In relation to the 9 vowel and 6-11 total it gives the splendid trinity of business balance, 8-9-11, combining the wisdom (11) and energy (11) of a keen organizer (6) and builder (8) with the power of a true publicity (9) man.

His total signature is higher than either his vowels or consonants, hence he has sufficient mental control and outlet to put his ideas into operation. The two trinities, 6-3-9 and 8-9-11, make it a strong, positive name.

There is no 7 digit in this signature but his original vowel of 7, in both middle and full name, gave him the inner consciousness of this vibration.

12. The total name is much higher than the birth path and is therefore abundantly able to handle the energy coming through.

The vowels being identical with the inner urge of 9 (birth path total) give him the *desire* to do what he came to do, and enable him to put his *soul* into his *work*.

The total signature of 6-11 is in harmony with the angle of his month (7) and day (8), which total 15 or 6. It gives him mastery (11) over this particular influence which colors each year's activities.

The unusual harmony and rhythm existing between Mr. Rockefeller's signature and his birth path, show the harmony between his field of action and his inner urge. Not that life has been a bed of roses, but that mastery over each succeeding problem has given new impetus for greater achievement.

"To him who hath, shall be given." Consider well what thou hast, and let it multiply accordingly.

CHAPTER XII

TWO NEGATIVES MAKE A POSITIVE

Every vibration consists of a forward movement with a reflex action but midway between these two extremes is the negative or neutral aspect. It is always the balance between two opposing forces that establishes a mean or harmony in any situation, but if the opposite poles be identical in character there is an entirely different resultant action than when such is not the case.

It is a rule of both algebra and English that "Two negatives make a positive." Whey you say "I *refuse* to *stay away,* you mean that you will *"go."* If you "will *not decline"* you will undoubtedly *accept.*

The one situation in a name where "two negatives make a positive" is where the Vowels and Full total signature are the same.

The individual is doing (total signature) just what he desires (vowels) to do, hence is apt to settle down into a smug state of self-satisfaction, or act in the opposite manner and be *overly* aggressive in his actions.

In order to find the true vibration of such an individual *we add these identical vibrations of vowel and full name and read the total so obtained.* Instead of the interpretation usually given to the name total, we would have its opposite aspect, as in these examples:

A 10 total and 10 vowel would be a negative 10 or a positive 20—alert (20) on the positive side, but timid (10), if he allows the negative influence to rule. (Each word followed by a number adds up to such vibration.)

A 2 total and 2 vowel would be a negative 2 or a positive 4. Since 2 is a natural lover of peace and public favor, this opposite aspect should result in a more positive frame of mind, although in reality this vibration is not one to be greatly desired if a higher influence can be obtained. Inlet and outlet would so abound with detail, red-tape, and routine, that there would be little freedom for creative expression.

A 3 total and 3 vowel is negative on the side of the 3, attracting all sorts of responsibility and requests for favors from those closely associated with him, which 99 times out of a 100 are not appreciated, or—he is a positive 6, rendering service in home and school, carrying graciously the responsibilities which greet him at nearly every turn. A negative 3 is beset with fear (3), but if he can see the humor (3) of the situation, he can step over onto the positive side of his vibration and use his dramatic (6) qualities to save the day.

A 4 total and 4 vowel is a positive 8. Using the positive aspect of this vibration he becomes a financial success through watching the details, putting time-saving and efficiency methods into play and being a keen buyer (8). Should he allow the negative influence to rule and neglect order and system in his work, he would undoubtedly find himself in a discomforting financial situation. His success (8) depends upon organization and a true sense of values.

A 5 total and a 5 vowel, a negative 5, makes this individual keenly susceptible to the influence of the opposite sex. It brings him problems (10) in sex as well as an unusually restless nature. If he wishes the true personal liberty and freedom of a 5 he must make an intelligent (10) use of his emotion (10) and not allow his heart to rule his head.

A 6 total and 6 vowel—negative 6 or positive 12 or 3,

attracts responsibilities and requests for favors somewhat similar to a negative 3 and positive 6. Any 3 must live on the principle of the triangle, which combines the 1-2-3 principle, if he wishes to succeed. This means that he must create (1), build (2) and put into use (3) some idea of his own. But if a 3 allows too many duties to absorb his time and attention so that he does not have an opportunity to act in a 3-fold manner himself, he is apt to be caught in the undertow, and instead of reaping the reward for his efforts, the benefit is apt to pass right over his head, into the path of someone else.

A 7 total and 7 vowel—negative 7 or positive 14-5, reverses the retiring quality of the 7. Here we have a fluent talker, an aggressive individual, one who can be unusually successful in the sale (a 5 quality) of real estate (7), or other nature (7) media. He is a true "go-getter" (go-getter has a 7 vowel and a 7 total), full of life (5) and enthusiasm, different in every way from the ordinary 7 name total.

An 8 total and 8 vowel is a negative 8 or positive 16-7. Instead of enjoying a large executive position and financial success which is due a true 8, this individual is often found in limited circumstances. He has a tendency to hold things to himself and turn people and things over in his mind. He grows suspicious, and instead of speaking his mind frankly, misinterprets the motives of others and is misunderstood himself. Any one operating under an 8-9-10-11 or 22 must express himself freely in a large way before the public if he wishes a reflex of good in his direction. An 8 who becomes self-centered or too introspective or aloof may get many original ideas, through the intuitive 7, but he will seldom have the finances to put them into operation. 8

calls for action (8) and the inhibitive 7, makes the 8 a dreamer instead of a doer.   Dreams are all right in their proper place, but action with executive tact and diplomacy, is imperative for an 8 if he does not wish to reverse his own forces.

A 9 total and 9 vowel would of course show a 9 consonant as well. Such individuals are apt to either be a genius in their line or go to extremes through lack of control of their strong emotions.   There are famous writers, lawyers and doctors who have this vibration in their name, but it is a dangerous one for an ordinary individual to handle. He must of necessity have a big (9) world (9) outlet if he wishes to maintain his balance and live in a constructive manner.

An 11 total and 11 vowel brings the 22 aspect into play and, with the consonant of 9, completes the trinity of balance on the high plane, 9-11-22.   This can hardly be said to be a negative condition, as it brings the high-powered triangle for professional success into uniformity of action. It is one of the strongest aspects of the double negative vibration.

Example—Al Smith

$$
\begin{array}{cccc}
1 & & 9 & = (10) \\
\text{A 1} & \text{Sm} & \text{i t h} & \\
3 & 1\ 4 & 2\ 8 & \\
\hline
& & 15 & \\
3 & & 6 & = (9) \\
1\ 3 & 1\ 4 & 9\ 2\ 8 & \\
\hline
& & 24 & \\
4 & & 6 & = (10)
\end{array}
$$

Add the 10 vowels and 10 total and we have 20—an alert (20) analyst (20) of any situation, with all the facts and figures at his finger tips. As Governor of New York and candidate for President, Mr. Smith's wide knowledge of the *facts* underlying state and national affairs, gave him that power which has been the admiration, even of his opponents.

CHAPTER XIII
WHY CHANGE YOUR NAME?

YOUR name is a good one because it represents you. Do not change it unless you can make it better.

Every change in name or signature opens a new door of opportunity for progress or retrogression. If you have changed your name through marriage or otherwise, note carefully whether you have raised or lowered your vibration. Changing your name will profit you nothing if you do not really express the positive characteristics of the new vibration and live up to the standard for which it stands.

At the same time, if you have really made an inner growth through your own efforts, circumstances will automatically shape themselves to give you a corresponding name. You will be elected President (11) of your company or Grand (8) Master (22) of your lodge.

The reason *why* you are here is shown by your birth date. If it is higher than the digit of your original name you have some big lessons to learn. You have come to gain honor and fame and strive for wealth and glory.

If your original name contains a master number (11 or 22) you are an old soul and have come to give out the knowledge already gained and to work in some public teaching capacity, through writing, lecturing or humanitarian lines, while the smaller digits of your birth path indicate the qualities you need to develop in order to make you a more rounded personality. You should care naught for wealth or fame; your mission is to deliver the message which comes to you through your inspirational and, psychic faculties.

What you really *are* at the present moment is revealed by your most frequent signature. It shows your present plane of action and understanding.

The only way by which you can master any lesson is by use of the mind with which you were endowed. If you are supposed to do a problem in algebra or geometry, something higher than 1-2-3—if your birth path contains 9, 11 or 22, it is plainly evident that in order to meet such problems you must have an intellect of equal capacity. Otherwise you are "up against it" and will have to do the best you can.

The most scientific method of gaining this understanding, if you have it not, is to raise the total value of your name to that of your birth path. After you have worn this vibration long enough the meaning thereof will sink into your subconscious mind and your intuition will reveal the path to follow.

Your Original Name an Index to Your True Nature

No matter how you may change your name, your original nature will always remain in the background, coloring your entire life. A typical example of such influence is that of Douglas Fairbanks, one of the most thrilling of movie actors. His original name, Douglas Ulmann, shows a 5 total in both vowels and consonants, with a full name of 10, while his birth date, May 23, 1883 (5+5+2=12=3), also contains a double 5 vibration, colored with the artistic 3. From four angles Douglas Fairbanks is a 5, twice in his original name and twice in his birth path. Throughout his career he has been a glowing example of the "go-getter"

vivid, active, experience-hunting 5 vibration, yet his present
name is lacking in any such digit total. The only 5 to be
found is the small consonant "n," scarcely sufficient to
furnish the thrills for his many-sided nature. He is one
of those individuals who will always be in the lead (10)
and "get there," no matter what mountains he has to climb.

Adjustment of Name

Your birth path represents the specific wave-length of
energy to which your entire life must be adjusted, hence by
putting your name in rhythm, you are harmonizing your
own forces.

Do not attempt, however, to change your own or another's
signature, until you are thoroughly familiar with the rules
which govern. In no field can it be said in greater truth,
"a little knowledge is a dangerous thing." The writer has
seen people with ordinarily successful vibrations who, thinking to benefit themselves, took another, and immediately
began to experience more acute reverses than before. In
any case there is always a period of adjustment until one
becomes accustomed to the new rhythm of forces set up.

You should not assume a name, no matter how scientific
it may be, unless it appeals to your own inner self, for in the
last analysis, your intuition should be your guide. Your
consciousness, not your numbers, is your controlling force.
Even though your outlet may be limited at the present time,
a developed consciousness and understanding of the higher
laws will enable you to break the boundaries and eventually
assume a different signature.

Rules of Rhythm for Name and Birth Date

Three important reasons for desiring to change your
signature are a greater enjoyment of health, happiness and

success. Considering the factors necessary in each one, the following points should be observed.

For health: Your total signature or outlet should be large enough to handle the vowels and consonants—your emotions and physical energy. High vowels and consonants with only a small name total generally make for a high strung temperament, either explosive or repressed, unless there be in the high numbers a complete trinity, such as 9-11-22 or 8-9-11, with which to handle the unusual amount of energy seeking to express.

A double master number in any position, such as an 11-11 vowel or 11-22 consonant or total, is too much of a good thing, unless the individual is an unusual person' with a large outlet before the public.

An extremely low consonant with a high vowel and total, or a very high consonant, with a low vowel and total, both indicate a lack of co-ordination between your physical, mental and emotional self. If your consonant is too low, you will either not have the time or physical vitality to encompass your desires and opportunities. If it is too high, you may not have the mental control to handle your emotions, but will be influenced before you know it by those who are able to get "under your skin."

There should be a reasonable balance of letters or total digits on all three planes—physical, mental and spiritual.

Where the 7 is entirely lacking there is apt to be a nervous temperament and need for greater relaxation.

In health, as in all other roads to power, it is well to have a trinity of balance in the name, such as 1-2-3, 8-9-10, 8-9-11 or 9-11-22.

For happiness: No one can appreciate anything outside of his own vibration, hence if you wish to be popular with

all types of people, every vibration should be present in
your name, or if not, then an 11 or 22 and a 1, representing
the beginning and end of the cycle, which include all others
between them.

Since no one can be truly happy, unless he is acting in
harmony with his inner urge, his total name should be in
harmony with that of his birth path, equal or higher in
value and if possible odd or even, as the case may be.

His vowels too, should be in harmony with his total
birth path, as then he can truly put his *soul* into his *work,*
and enjoy it.

For success: In the highest measure, some trinity should
be present in the name, especially the fundamental principle
of balance represented by the 1-2-3 principle, the power to
create (1), build (2) and put into complete form or use
(3) your own ideas.   In the high numbers 1 is found in
10 or 11, 2 in 8 or 22 and 3 in 9.

The word *business* incorporates in its vowels of 8, consonants of 10 and total of 9 the 3 principles necessary for
individual success in any line—the idea (10) financed and
organized (8 qualities), with the proper publicity (9) to
put it over.   If you are lacking in any one of these attributes
you will need the assistance of someone else to supply the
missing link.

For specialized branches of endeavor, the 3-6-9 trinity
is an aid to literary, artistic or humanitarian expression, the
1-5-7 to scientific or philosophical pursuits.

If you desire to wield an influence in your world, your
total name should be a strong one, as subconsciously a high
vibrating individual resents taking advice from a lower
one, no matter how scientific or correct it may be.

Your consonants should be neither too high nor too low.

If too low, others are apt to load you with more than your share of responsibilities; if too high, in spite of your strong personality, you are subject to flattery from the opposite sex. You may strongly deny the accusation, yet we scarcely feel that this will materially alter the situation.

A total signature in harmony with the angle of your month and day (your month and day added together), not forgetting that it should be as high or higher than your total birth path digit, will help to maintain the proper mental attitude in the handling of your affairs.

Harmony between your name and birth path, or between your environment and your inner urge, should produce improved results from every angle. When you have adjusted your inner to your outer self, you are then in a position to bring your business into line, and choose a name for your product or corporation in harmony with your own vibrations.

Choosing a Nom de Plume

In choosing a name for a professional career, care should be taken to make it fit the particular field you intend to enter, not forgetting to harmonize it with your birth path total.

All of the digits should be present in your name in some manner if you wish to influence all classes of people. If such is not possible, then see to it that you have an 11 or a 22 and also a 1, and thereby you will include all others.

Striking examples of those who have risen to fame following a change in name would fill several volumes, two world figures being Mark Twain, the famous humorist, author of "Huckleberry Finn" and "Tom Sawyer," and

Sarah Bernhardt, the most famous actress of all time.

The original name of Mark Twain was Samuel Langhorne Clemens, which had a vowel vibration of 9-3-1, totaling 4; a consonant vibration of 8-1-7, totaling 7, and a total vibration of 8-4-8, totaling 20. Not a very auspicious name for an author.

Under his pen name Mark Twain had a vowel vibration of 1-10 (11), a consonant vibration of 6-3 (9), and a total vibration of 7-22 (7-22). In his consonants he gained the complete trinity of literary and artistic expression, 6-3-9, while his total digits show the trinity of balanced creative expression on the high plane 11-22-9. The 1 of his first vowel and the 22 of his last name enabled him to reach all classes, as between them are found all other vibrations. A splendid name, giving him inspiration, personality, and a big understanding of the needs of the average mind, while the strong 8 of his real nature came through with the necessary analytical qualities to make his creations real and to place a true value on their monetary worth.

Sarah Bernhardt was christened Rosine Bernard, which latter name shows a vowel vibration of 2+6, totaling 8, a consonant vibration of 6-11 and a total vibration of 8+8=16=7. Her birth date was October 22, 1844, 10-22-8, giving a total of 22-9, the most perfect trinity of numbers possible for an actress.

In the name of Sarah Bernhardt she maintained her original vowel vibration of 2+6=8, had a consonant vibration of 9+3=12=3, and a total of 2+9=11. Here the 9 of her last name met the 9 of her birth path, giving her full and free artistic expression in a large way, while the 11 total gave her unbounded inspiration with

which to sway the public mind and make her an outstanding (11) figure in the realm of dramatic (2) art (9).
Her full name (11) was now on the same plane with
the 22 and 9 of her birth and in harmony with both. Her
powerful inner self shown by the vowel vibration of 8
gave her that eternal driving force which enabled her to
conquer fate. A strong, indomitable soul she was, whose
glory will not fade, and whose accomplishments were truly
those of a 22-9 vibration.

CHAPTER XIV
VOCATION—BUSINESS

THE total digit of your birth, with its respective digits of month, day and year, shows the character attributes that you have come to develop, which when acquired will attract the work calling for the exercise of such qualities. The sooner you make them a part of yourself, the sooner will your right work find you.

While the final digit of birth should be given paramount consideration, the digits of month, day and year play an important part in the choice of a vocation, particularly during the periods which they govern.

Your Right Sphere

Suppose your birth date were March 1st, 1899, the digits of which are 3-1-9, totaling 13 or 4. This does not necessarily mean that you should be an office manager or an automobile mechanic, both of which vocations can be successfully handled by a 4, but it does mean that you are to develop your intellect and obtain a first-class education along the lines of music, art, law, healing or other humanitarian calling, remembering that 1 always accentuates the qualities of the other digits to which it is related.

During the first 27 years of your life, governed by the 3 vibration, you should study music, dramatic art, build up your physical constitution and engage in all kinds of activities which will develop your self-expression.

Between the age of 27 and 54 you are under the influence of the 1 vibration, when you should begin to stand on your own feet, discard the advice of others and act on your own intuition. This is the time for you to do creative work, write your own compositions, organize, manage and

promote your own plays, and become the brilliant com-
poser or builder along artistic lines which the total of 4
enables you to be.   When a 4 "delivers the goods" he
builds (4) a reputation which will remain with him forever.

The more aggressive you are during this cycle of 1, the
more "do and dare" spirit you put into your efforts, the
sooner will you "arrive" in the 9 of your year,—full and
free artistic expression in a universal way, with opportunity
for extended travel, fame and the good things of life,—
the natural reflex action from the creative efforts of your
previous cycle.

Therefore, in choosing a life work take into consideration *all* of your birth path digits, but give preference to
the grand total.   If the work you do is not listed here,
find the number value of its dominant word, and see
whether you have a like vibration.   While there have been
many famous lawyers in the professional 7, law itself
totals 9, while lawyer totals 3.   3 and 9 are also the art
and humanitarian numbers.   With both of these digits in
your birth path, look to the remaining numbers and to the
original name in order to determine in which branch of
self-expression you should throw your creative efforts.

A few occupations calling for the particular qualities
of the different vibrations are shown in the following
list of

Vocations

1. Inventor, designer, promoter, aviator, superintend-
ent, teacher, writer or lecturer along metaphysical and
occult lines—creative work in avenues indicated by other
digits of the birth path or name.

2. Statistician, secretary, collector, arbitrator, diplomat, actor.

3. Artist, musician, lawyer, nurse, dietitian, physician, nature-cure specialist, writer, entertainer, manager of hotel, restaurant or beauty parlor, salesman of advertising, drugs, art goods, musical instruments, cosmetics, groceries, artisan in any line. Happy in those avenues which make for health, beauty or comfort. Should avoid positions calling for too close confinement, long hours or prolonged attention to detail. Individual self-expression is absolutely essential to success.

4. A builder, either on the physical or mental plane, a mechanic, draftsman, architect, electrician, manufacturer, efficiency expert, office executive, stenographer, clerk, bookkeeper, accountant, dealer in coal, brick and building materials. Any routine business requiring a combination of intellect, skill, perseverance, endurance and energy.

5. Investigator, detective, character analyst, vocational employment director, writer on scientific, occult or metaphysical subjects, a rejuvenator on all planes—the traveling salesman, vaudeville player or noted psychology lecturer. Must have speed and action; is not happy in routine work but must have the opportunity to make his own schedule and exercise his own intuitive powers in the handling of any situation.

6. The home-maker, business man, teacher, educator, writer or public speaker, hotel manager, head of hospital or other public institution, nurse, doctor, interior decorator, florist. Must be cheerful and happy in service for others in order to be successful.

7. The professional man, supreme in his own realm, one who runs his own business and has his own established

center of activity, successful in law, dentistry, real estate, horticulture, agriculture, mining, or as preacher, teacher and writer. Dislikes manual labor, does best in an atmosphere of refinement and culture. Perfection, finish and quality are required rather than size or quantity.

8. Engineer, banker, broker, corporation lawyer, executive, organizer, business or corporation head,—builders on all planes where keen discrimination, good judgment, perseverance, tact and driving qualities are needed. Also make good actors.

9. Artist, musician, actor, physician, healer, lawyer, beauty expert, writer, lecturer, humanitarian worker, world traveler, also successful in horticulture, floriculture and landscape gardening. Must have free artistic expression in a large way.

11. Inspirational speaker or writer, lecturer, preacher, promoter, sales manager, leader in public affairs and in the lines indicated by other digits of birth path or name.

22. Executive, diplomat, arbitrator, actor, librarian, business manager, statesman, corporation lawyer, humanitarian adviser of the highest order, active in practical philanthropic projects. Often found as bookkeeper, clerk or accountant, but should realize that such occupation is the limited aspect of the 22 vibration. He should fit himself for public service, study dramatic art, public speaking, character analysis and vocational guidance and prepare himself to act in some advisory capacity in an unlimited environment.

The Proper Business Medium

Having decided to enter business for yourself, what is the next important point to be considered? The proper selling medium.

The story of John D. Rockefeller's success in oil is told in Chapter X. There were several points of vibratory contact between his own name and his main "line." He promoted a medium having the same vibration as his vowels, while his business name and his own signature carried the same values.

Henry Ford rose to fame with the Ford car. His name totals 5, made up of 7 plus 7, totaling 14 or 5. Automobile totals 5, but when he had perfected it to the point where it deserved a name, he called it the Ford (7) car (4), which together totals 11, a master number, making it stand supreme in its own field. Mr. Ford was born on July 30, 1863, the digits of his birth path being 7-3-9, totaling 19 or 10. This shows plainly that as an inventor Mr. Ford was in his "right pew," working in a vibration identical with his name. Through adhering to his own ideas he evolved an article of superior merit, as its name reveals, while he has wooed still further the vibratory forces of large success in the business name of Ford Motor Company, which is made up of the digits 7-9-6, totaling 22, the highest vibration of all.

Location

If your name totals 22, you should do well in Boston, which has the same vibration. If your signature is only 4, Washington, D. C., would be a good location. A city whose total number value is the same as your own will be active in those lines which you are able to handle.

You must remember that before trying to adjust yourself to a location numerologically, you must first adjust your name to your birth path. You will always find opportunity for growth and development in a city having the same vibration as your date of birth. If you have a name in harmony with your birth, and then settle down in a city with a like vibration, you have two points of harmony which should make for assured success.

If you have a choice of street numbers, one which is in harmony with your present signature should control, not forgetting that your own name and business name should be odd or even, according to the digit of birth.

You should also do well in a city whose vowel vibration is the same as your total name. In such instance you *are* what they desire, and it is up to you to give satisfaction.

The Triangle and the Square in Business

There is said to be no perfection without the reflection of the Trinity, symbolized by the triangle, or the 1-2-3 principle, yet if this statement be true there must be some law corroborative of this fact, which if observed, should make for success in all lines of activity.

As the tree grows in size and stature, adding one ring each year, through the 3-fold process of breathing through its leaves, extracting strength from the earth through its roots and pushing outward from its center, so is this 3-fold principle of growth necessary in every perfected project.

1 or the creative idea, plus 2 or the materials for its growth, plus 3 or the pushing outward into visible expression, brings the triangle into the square or fourth principle —the use to which the completed unit is put. 1 plus 2 plus 3 plus 4 equals 10, the beginning of a new cycle of expression. We cannot pass from one number to another, from 3 to 4, from 4 to 5 or from 99 to 100 without returning and appropriating the creative 1. Neither can we progress from our present situation on to a better one without the introduction of a new idea.

Proof of this law is found in numbers themselves. Beginning with 4, every third number by occult addition (including both the first and last number) adds up to some number which reduces to 10. 1 to 7 inclusive add up to 28 or 10, 1 to 10 inclusive add to 55 or 10, 1 to 13 inclusive add to 91 or 10, etc.

Thus does the creative 1 always stand alone—the motive power behind each group of 3, whose presence is needed every time a forward step is made.

Your idea squared and put into use, a new triangle immediately evolves in the 5, 6 and 7.

5. Here you must introduce some clever idea for the sale (5) of your project. In placing it upon the market you learn the reaction of the public, which may necessitate some further improvement in the original article. The experience gained here teaches you that in

6. You need to establish an educational program, both for the public and your own organization if you would render the greatest service to the community and enjoy correspondingly large return.

7. Having perfected an article of distinctive merit and established a quality service, so that your project is the best of its kind in the community, you have reached the cycle of physical perfection, whence you are ready to evolve into the larger square of 8.

8. Here your idea is introduced through other organizations or subsidiary corporations. The business expansion thus obtained and the larger executive duties, develop tact, diplomacy, keen fighting qualities, and a knowledge that after all the Golden Rule is the most scientific principle on which to build a lasting business success. In truth it

is nothing but the statement of the law of vibration. "Do unto others as you would have others do unto you" is the forward movement with the reflex action, and if the doing comes first, the proper results are bound to follow.

9. In 9 man comes into the enjoyment of the previous efforts made, and if each succeeding step was built safe and sound he should have the money, time and opportunity to carry out a greater publicity (9) program than ever before, and travel the world (9) o'er in search of another new idea (10).

CHAPTER XV

SELLING TIPS

NOTE: *When we speak of a 1 or a 2 individual, we mean one in whom such number is the predominating digit, whether in individual or full name totals, added strength being shown if it also appears in date of birth.*

SUCCESSFUL salesmanship depends on a forehand knowledge of your customer. This can easily be obtained from his business card by use of the table in Chapter III.

1. If you are selling to a 1, an individual whose first vowel is "a" or whose total name is 10, be sure that your article is *different* from the ordinary run of things. He wants something new, novel or intellectual, with distinctly progressive features.

2. If you are selling to a 2, be sure that you are perfectly groomed before entering the "inner sanctuary." He desires those things which will give him comfort, ease and prestige. Use tact and diplomacy in your approach, with just a touch of expert flattery, and it will help you land the order.

3. If you are selling a 3, be enthusiastic about something which makes an appeal to the eye, conveying the idea of beauty, comfort, health or pleasure. To get his name on the dotted line, invite him out to a first-class dinner but close the deal between the last two courses. If you give him time to think it over he will be apt to change his mind. 3 can also be reached through his sympathies.

4. If you are selling a 4, make your visit short and snappy; he has no patience with social calls. Be sure your logic is sane and sound and your article worth double

the money. He cares not for beauty or style; the thing he buys must be practical, workable, durable, and guaranteed to last.

5. If you are selling a 5, breeze in with a cheerful smile and pique his curiosity. He wants to know all there is to know, so keep him guessing. Give him a brief character sketch of himself, from his face, his head, his hand or his name, and you will have his whole attention. Then with speed and agility present your topic. It must have a human appeal, afford a new experience or present some unusual departure from the regular scheme of things. He is interested in life and in staying young; so make your attack accordingly.

6. If you are selling a 6, one with a first vowel "o," a last name Smith, or some other form of this vibration, you must be able to hold your own in any argument. He is interested most in those things which make for beauty and comfort in his home, the better education of his children or the more efficient conduct of his business. Your article must not only be worth the money but must have an esthetic air about it, something useful, beautiful and of high quality.

7. If you are selling a 7, be careful! He has a decided mind of his own, and of all vibrations his is the hardest to influence. Ask his advice first, get an expression from him and then counter with your idea. Present your proposition complete in every detail, dwell on its perfection, finish and quality. Never mind about the quantity; he wants the *best* or none at all.

8. If you are selling an 8, be sure to radiate an atmosphere of success and prosperity yourself. He is interested in constructive things which are practical, at-

tractive, elegant, and generous in proportions. Convince him that your idea put into practice in his business will increase his output, strengthen his finances, provide jusr compensation to his employes and make him an outstanding figure in his world.

9. If you are selling a 9 and have a pleasing air about you, you will have a sympathetic listener, provided your project is sufficiently large in proportions to engage his attention. He is interested in those things which pertain to music, art and self-expression on a large scale. He is also the strong advocate of all things which make for better health, more wealth or increased enjoyment of life from every angle. Anything which has a human interest appeal will meet with a favorable reception if you are large enough yourself to present it in world terms.

11. If you are selling an 11, you must be inspired with a big, new and wonderful idea. You must be enthusiastic, yet calm and psychic enough to get his psychic reaction to your proposition. He is interested in those things which will give him greater inspiration, more influence over other people, greater opportunity to expound his ideas, and an established place in the public eye.

22. If you are selling a 22 you must have a proposition of merit, practical as well as idealistic, combining reason with human sympathy and proof with your philosophy. Give your prospect a world view, and direct his attention to this opportunity for public service. Even though he be a bookkeeper or clerk, he knows very well that there are larger things in store for him, with international diplomacy topping the list.

The first point to observe in applying the stimulus for each individual is the *first vowel* of his name. This is one of his strongest pivotal centers. Ascertain however, if he is called by his first or his last name. His most frequent appellation is the base on which to work.

With respect to the vowels, we consider "y" a vowel when sounded, as in Clyde, Mary or Henry, but a consonant when silent as in May or Raymond.

CHAPTER XVI
FRIENDS AND MARRIAGE

WHY do you take an immediate liking to some individuals and feel a natural antipathy toward others? It is a matter of vibration. Just as the chemical elements of calcium and carbon have an affinity for each other and as oil and water do not mix, so do our vibrations attract similar ones and repel others.

Your Friends

Your friends are those who think as you do, feel as you do or have a like ambition.

When you meet a person with a *vowel vibration the same* as your own there is an immediate bond of sympathy and understanding, and the more individual vowels you have in common, the stronger will be the attraction. Your subconscious selves have a desire for expression along the same lines which makes for real enjoyment.

One whose *consonants are the same* as yours will be a splendid friend for your idle hours, as the outward things of life have a kindred appeal.

One whose *full name is the same* or in the same trinity of expression makes a splendid business companion. Your minds register on the same plane, whether in work or study.

One whose total *birth digit is the same* as yours is in your present grade of school. You may have come from widely separated localities with a totally different background, yet you are here now for a common purpose and should get along famously together, tackling the same problems with co-operation, sympathy and courage.

One whose *name has the same vibration as your birth* has something to teach you, provided he is on your mental plane. The probability is that when you meet such a person you will find that one of his birth digits is present in your name, and that you will both benefit from such association.

A strong point of contact frequently noted is where one individual *is* (through his total name) what the other *desires* (in his vowels). A person *whose total vowels equal your full name* will attach himself to you and remain there unshaken whether you notice him or not. You have something that he wants. After a time you become so accustomed to the situation that you begin to take it as a matter of course. If he has nothing in his name to answer your vowels or birth digit you will be doing all the giving and he all the receiving, but *if his name equals your vowels, then you are complements of each other* and there will be an opportunity for splendid growth through such a friendship. Each has an inner knowledge of the other's destiny and at the same time is expressing in his full character the other's subconscious desires.

Marriage

In order to have an ideal home life there must be some harmony between the individual vibrations. Marriage itself tends to bring this about through the wife taking the husband's name. In addition thereto there are several ways by which the atmosphere can be made more happily harmonious.

One splendid assurance of genuine pleasure is where husband and wife have the same vowel total. With the same vibrations there are like desires; they enjoy the same things, and enjoy each other, the chief danger being that they are apt to settle down in such snug self-satisfaction that their real growth may be retarded. They should endeavor to extend their interests beyond their own family circle and continue to grow, together.

Those with the same total name vibrations can co-operate splendidly, as their minds are on the same plane and their activities can be made of a like enjoyable nature. If they are not the same but are in the same trinity, it makes for a splendid partnership, as each has the qualities which the other lacks, both being necessary for complete success.

Those with the same birth path have the same qualities of character to develop; they can succeed in similar occupations; in fact, they can go all through life together, with sympathy and tolerance for the other fellow, as they have the same shortcomings themselves. This is a very successful marriage vibration.

For those who have 11s or 22s in their *original* names it would appear that the law of complements should rule. They are already old souls, and if they have elsewhere a 1 in their name they are undoubtedly in their last earth cycle. Their progress may have been over different routes and hence their present lesson not the same, yet each is the ideal expression of the other's heart's desire, which makes for a most satisfying, enduring companionship. It may not have the zest in mutual accomplishment which is found when the birth paths are the same, as each now has his own particular destiny to fulfill, nor the thrill of pleasure enjoyed when the vowels are identical, yet there is an inner feeling that each is helping the other to complete his last initiation in this cycle, which unselfish efforts will eventually register in a subsequent change of name, bringing their inner desires closer together through a harmony of vowels.

Another most happy marriage relation is where each one has in his original name the birth vibrations of the other.

Whenever a woman marries a man whose surname has the same vibration as her Year—which is the rule in the majority of cases, she has attracted an important lesson. No matter what his qualities may be, he has something to teach her. The same adjustment may need to be made if his surname or full signature is the same as her total birth path.

One of the strongest points of harmony for mutual companionship, year in and year out, is where the Month and Day of each add to the same total. August 6 (8 plus 6 is 14 or 5) and February 3 (2 plus 3 is 5) are instances of this character. This gives the same influence each month and year, throughout their lives. If one wants to travel, the other will arrange his affairs and go at the same time. When one wants to stay, that will be the desire of the other. With this splendid point of agreement, they should be able to adjust all other differences and enjoy life to the full.

CHAPTER XVII
TWO-MINUTE SKETCHES
From the Number of Your Sign in the Zodiac

THE characteristics of each vibration being transmitted by its digit to whatever such number applies, it naturally follows that the digit which determines the position of each sign in the zodiac will cause its particular qualities to be reflected in such sign.

Brief character sketches from an astrological standpoint are given here, showing how the two sciences of Astrology and Numerology correlate and support each other. A more complete treatment of the subject from this angle is found in "Finding Yourself By Numbers."

Number Features of the 12 Signs

1. ARIES—March 22 to April 20. Symbol, the ram. First fire sign, governing the *head* and *face.*

This influence gives an emotional nature and the strong 1 characteristics of aggressiveness, independence, courage, push, energy, originality, determination, keen intellect and intuition. The Aries individual is a natural leader in any field, interested in psychology, metaphysics and the occult. Because of his great desire to rule he can never be driven or forced.

His adverse characteristics, common to the 1 vibration, are impatience, anger, stubbornness, selfishness, egotism, arrogance and jealousy. He should cultivate patience and concentration, avoid worry and anxiety and learn to obey the "still small voice" within.

2. TAURUS—April 21 to May 21. Symbol, the bull. First earth sign, governing the *neck* and *throat.*

This influence gives the individual a receptive, reserved, conservative "stay-on-the-ground" nature, with geniality, sympathy, a splendid memory and large talent in imitation. He is fond of books and reading, close-mouthed regarding own affairs, yet magnetic and well liked. Interested mainly in those things which make for the satisfaction of the senses. Has strong will (2) yet can be influenced by arousing his sympathy. Excels in literature and mathematics. Is practical and constructive in his business operations.

His 2 defects are stubbornness, strong passions, jealousy, sarcasm, with a selfish love of ease and comfort. He should cultivate self-control, patience and an interest in the higher things of life. Should build up self-esteem and work in those lines where he can express his social nature, or gather and correlate information for others, where originality is not required.

3. GEMINI—May 22 to June 21. Symbol, the twins. First air sign, governing the *arms* and *hands*.

This influence has the qualities of both 1 and 2, making it changeable, imaginative, highstrung. It indicates a dual personality, genial, sympathetic, generous, yet at other times the exact opposite. Full of clever ideas, versatile, adaptable, with energy, wit and sarcasm. It combines the creative ability of 1 with the tact of 2 and transforms mental images into concrete realities. It gives a love of the beautiful in nature and art, with fluency of speech and a magnetic personality. In order to be happy there must be variety and perfect freedom of expression; too much routine dampens the enthusiasm and brings the adverse nature into play.

The 3 defects evidence themselves in a restless disposition, going to extremes. He has plenty of ideas but lacks the continuity to bring them into complete expression. His independence leads him to override conventionality, and his strong passions make him susceptible to the wiles of the opposite sex. He should associate with people of strength and poise, learn to make decisions quickly, cultivate will power and develop his higher self.

4. CANCER—June 22 to July 22. Symbol, the crab. First water sign, governing the *breasts*.

This influence gives strong lungs and good breathing power, with the 4 qualities of mechanical and constructive ability, business sagacity, determination, perseverance, economy and painstaking effort. The Cancer individual succeeds well in business and manufacturing lines or in intellectual pursuits. He can be ruled through kindness but resents compulsion.

His defects are self-limitation, criticism, too great economy, and an over-cautious nature. He reasons himself out of his good intentions. It is very important for him to gain a good education if he does not always wish to be in a subservient position. He should associate with those of broad views and large interests.

5. LEO—July 23 to August 23. Symbol, the lion. Second fire sign, governing the *heart*.

This influence gives a strong emotional love nature, with the charming, impulsive, fearless characteristics of the 5 vibration. The Leo individual is .. splendid entertainer, full of youth and exuberant spirits, versatile, adaptable, with a pleasing and magnetic personality; very fond of the opposite sex. He must have personal freedom at all cost, the keynote of 5. Although he acts almost solely upon his intuition and is somewhat hasty in judgment, he is better fitted to rule than be ruled.

His defects, found in a 5, are aversion to study, quick anger, a selfish disregard for others, being ruled by his passions. He should develop will power and learn to take responsibilities, which will bring out his latent powers and give him the authority which he craves.

6. VIRGO—August 24 to September 23. Symbol, the virgin. Second earth sign, governing the *digestive organs.*

This influence gives the strong mother, home-loving nature of the 6 vibration, with great talent in educational and literary lines. While it is materialistic in some respects and rather exclusive, when the spiritual nature is once developed the individual becomes a leader in all things which make for better homes, health and education. He is a protector of the rights of others rather than an originator or promoter, and succeeds well in either business or professional lines, especially as a writer, teacher or lecturer.

His faults are those of a reverse or negative 6—he talks too much and either refuses to assume responsibility or tries to take the burden of the world upon his shoulders. He should direct his attention to matters of health and education, and get into some position which *requires* expression on his part, when he will not have such a keen desire to criticise the efforts of others.

7. LIBRA—September 24 to October 23. Symbol, the balance. Second air sign, governing the *reins,* the *kidneys* and reproductive system.

This influence gives strong intuition, with a love of refinement, beauty, luxury, and a desire for knowledge along many lines. The 7 attributes are strongly marked in the sensitive, persistent, positive nature, which finishes in a careful manner whatever one undertakes. Being guided by his intuitive faculties, this individual is gifted with remarkable foresight and reacts quickly to atmosphere and environment. He is fond of scientific and philosophical subjects, psychology, metaphysics and the mysteries of the occult, and could excel as a linguist, musician, writer or lecturer, or in any line requiring continuity of thought, discrimination, precision, and an inspirational insight into the nature of people or things.

The 7 defects which appear in this sign are egotism, pride and too great susceptibility to flattery and praise. It is hard for him to express what he feels. He should study public speaking, art, literature, character analysis, or anything which will develop his powers of self-expression. He should also take regular periods for rest and relaxation away from crowds and excitement.

8. SCORPIO—October 24 to November 22. Symbol, the scorpion. Second water sign, governing the *groin* or *generative organs*.

This influence gives to the individual the courage, confidence, dignity, keen discrimination, executive ability and energetic nature of the 8 vibration. Good judgment, practicality, diplomacy, tact, tenacity, together with a strong personality, make him an excellent judge, critic, politician, executive, public speaker or writer, wielding power with tongue or pen.

Adverse characteristics are criticism, intolerance, procrastination and an inclination to domineer and rule by fear. He allows suspicion and jealousy to blunt his powers. Should overcome any inferiority complex (another name for jealousy) and know that he will attract his own when he is that thing himself.

9. SAGITTARIUS—November 23 to December 22. Symbol, the archer. Third fire sign, governing the *thighs*.

This influence gives the individual a sympathetic, whole-souled love (9) nature with energy, enthusiasm, and a genial, happy, jovial disposition. He likes everything on a large scale, and the first thing he is apt to do, when he falls heir to a legacy, is to tour the world, entertain his friends, give to his pet philanthropies, and then, if he has any money left, start a bank account. He has good chances for success as a musician, lawyer, actor, physician, preacher or teacher.

Some of his adverse characteristics are "nerves," quick temper, and the inability to make allowances for others. Should be careful to marry on his own intellectual and spiritual plane. Should learn to relax and conserve his energies.

10. CAPRICORN—December 23 to January 20. Symbol, the goat. Third earth sign, governing the *knees*.

This influence gives the individual an independent, executive, forceful bearing, a high moral nature, ingenuity, and the organizing ability which naturally falls within the 10 vibration. He is a good manager, positive in his opinions, courageous in surmounting obstacles, public-spirited, self-confident, and makes an excellent teacher, writer or leader in any field, always keeping one foot firmly on the earth, no matter how high his aspirations climb.

Adverse characteristics are self-conceit, self-consciousness, egotism and a domineering attitude. He should have a thorough, all-round education and should associate with broad-minded and tolerant people.

11. AQUARIUS—January 21 to February 19. Symbol, the water-bearer. Third air sign, governing the *limbs*.

This influence gives the individual a highly strung nervous system, keen intuition, good judgment, and a pleasing hypnotic eye. He is an excellent judge of human nature, a good politician, convincing speaker, blessed with a saving sense of humor. He is ambitious for knowledge and eminently fitted to pass it on through writing, lecturing or other public avenues. He should direct his large imagination toward one end until that goal is achieved. He cares nothing for precedent; he is an 11 all over—always interested in making a *new beginning*, doing everything in a different way than it was ever done before.

Adverse characteristics are procrastination, prevarication, indolence, always seeking advice but accepting none; is apt to have an exaggerated ego. Should study metaphysics, psychology, character analysis and the occult sciences. Should cultivate punctuality and self-reliance and learn to be a good listener.

12. PISCES—February 20 to March 21. Symbol, the fishes. Third water sign, governing the *feet* and *ankles*.

12 is the number of numerical completion. Its digits total 3, complete individual self-expression, with all the positive characteristics of the 1 and 2. The Pisces individual is an apt illustration of the 3 vibration, showing skill in art, with splendid opportunities for success in scientific, inventive and literary fields. He is magnetic, attractive, with an inspiring and helpful nature, a good observer, generous, sincere, sympathetic, but one who tends strictly to his own affairs. He is a great seeker after knowledge, desiring to know the reason why in every situation.

His adverse characteristics are lack of self-esteem, worrying about things which never happen and carrying a "chip" on his shoulder. He should learn to rely on his inner self, should maintain a cheerful attitude and choose a vocation which calls for creative self-expression.

The Cusps

Those born in the cusps partake of the characteristics of both signs. "Cusps," in astrology, are the beginning or first entrance of any "house" in the determination of nativities.

1. Aries and Taurus (1 and 2)—April 19-25.
2. Taurus and Gemini (2 and 3)—May 20-26.
3. Gemini and Cancer (3 and 4)—June 21-27.
4. Cancer and Leo (4 and 5)—July 22-28.
5. Leo and Virgo (5 and 6)—August 23-28.
6. Virgo and Libra (6 and 7)—September 23-29.
7. Libra and Scorpio (7 and 8)—October 23-29.
8. Scorpio and Sagittarius (8 and 9)—November 22-28.
9. Sagittarius and Capricorn (9 and 10)—December 21-27.
10. Capricorn and Aquarius (10 and 11)—January 20-26.
11. Aquarius and Pisces (11 and 12)—February 19-25.
12. Pisces and Aries (12 and 1)—March 21-27.

CHAPTER XVIII
BEST DAYS, COLORS and MUSICAL KEY

YOUR BEST DAYS are good days for everyone, but on those days which have the same vibration as your total birth digit the forces of the universe are especially harmonious to any new undertaking you may wish to promote.

At such times you should make a careful note of the impressions received, as events of a similar character extending over a period of several weeks or months are strongly indicative of the course you should follow. If adverse conditions appear, seek out the root and cause and let your inner self reveal the secret. Strengthen your own forces by sending out a strong current of good-will to all the universe, and by the law of reflex action it is bound to return with blessings in its wake.

To find the vibration of any day, add the digits of month, day and year together, and reduce the final total. The only exception is when 11 or 22 appear and make a combination total. In such case, if your birth path be 11-4, your *best days* are all those which total either 11 or 4.

July 31, 1926, shows a total digit of 11-9. July is the 7th month. The digits of 31 added are 4. The digits of 1926 (1-9-2-6) total 18, while 18 (1-8) totals 9. While we never add the day or the month to the year in order to obtain an 11 or 22, when the *first two* digits of the date (month and day) total 11 or 22, they show the possibility of leadership in the realm of the year vibration.

August 11, 1926, shows the digits 8-11-9. Here we add the 8 and 9, which gives us 17 or 8, and allow the

11 to stand intact. This gives a total birth digit of 11-8.

August 9, 1939, shows the digits 8-9-22. Here we add the 8 and 9, giving us 17 and a total digit of 8-22.

Every day can be made a winner if you live in harmony with its dominant note. You can easily form the habit of noting its value and, whenever *your* vibration appears, making a special effort, through the color of your dress and general activities, to tune in with the universal forces.

On a 1 *day*—Start something, be aggressive, act on your intuition, heed not the advice of others.

On a 2 *day*—Be receptive to suggestions, learn to co-operate, try to get the other fellow's point of view, be observing, study and collect your materials for a more complete expression tomorrow.

On a 3 *day*—Express your own individual self in some creative way. Be happy,—make seven people smile and you will take a new lease on life.

On a 4 *day*—Rise early, hum a march tune, walk briskly to the office and get your mail out on schedule time. Work done well today will give you more satisfaction than any kind of a vacation.

On a 5 *day*—Be active and enthusiastic, investigate your business and social prospects, study human nature, analyze yourself and your surroundings and generate new pep into your environment.

On a 6 *day*—Look after your business interests, your health and education, and surprise your wife with a box of candy, or, better still, tell her you will stay home with the children tonight while she goes out for a little recreation.

On a 7 *day*—Finish up the odds and ends, then hie yourself to the country and take things easy; listen to your "still small voice" and you will get a new idea for business tomorrow.

On an 8 day—Be a real executive, organize your forces, drive yourself and your business with justice and tact. Render a real service in a big way and you will be blessed with equally large returns.

On a 9 day—If you have any artistic talent, prepare to shine today in some public performance. Send out good will to all the world; hold not a single grudge; find something in every one to commend, voicing your appreciation thereof in words. This is a *love* day, but you must first send out the vibration if you would have love in return. Money likewise should appear if you are generous and philanthropic in your giving.

On an 11 day—You will get an inspiration; listen to it and make a new beginning. Deal with the public, let your light shine, and give out the knowledge you have to others.

On a 22 day—Lay big plans,—the sky is your limit,— but make your ideas practical. Be energetic, organize, advise, yet do not fail to keep your word, for the adverse aspect is laziness and glowing promises unfulfilled. This is the day when earth and heaven meet and the best time ever to build your dreams into concrete realities.

Colors

Color is one of the primary mediums for transmitting the characteristics of each digit to people or things. To find the vibration of any color, add the letter values of the word.

While the colors of your name can be worn attractively, those of your birth path have a much stronger and a greater health-giving influence, as they carry the vibrations you have come to develop. Choose from the colors of your birth date the one most in harmony with the digit of the day and let it play a dominant note in your dress and room furnishings.

If you are in business, feature the color of the day in your window display.

A few colors with their number vibrations are shown below:

1—Crimson, flame.
2—Salmon, gold.
3—Rose, orchid.
4—Blue, green, indigo.
5—Lemon, pink.
6—Scarlet, orange, heliotrope, wine, gray, henna.
7—Brick, purple.
8—Mauve, tan, buff, canary.
9—Red, brown, taupe, lavender.
11—White, black, yellow, violet, dark green, dark blue.
22—Cream.

The same law applies to flowers, perfumes, fruits, foods, trees, gems, musical instruments or anything else in the universe. You are the magnetic center of your world, attracting "your own"—those things which have the same vibration as your date of birth being of primary importance, those of your name a close second.

Music

Music is the harmonious vibration of sound. Sound is not music unless there be a definite rhythm—a regular recurrence of accents within a certain interval or period of time.

Each note in the scale, in common with each letter of the alphabet, and all else in this universe, has its number value, according to its numerical position in the unit of measurement in which it is found.

If all the digits are present in your name you have the entire scale of life on which to play. But if certain notes are lacking, you are like the piano with the ivory missing on certain keys. You may know how the music ought to sound, you may have your ideas of how delightful it would be if the other person would tune in with your viewpoint, but it will be much more difficult to produce the desired harmony.

No one can appreciate anything outside of his own vibrations. Therefore, see to it that you have a chord—a trinity in your name, or that all important vibrations are present. Then polish your keys and play your life's symphony in the rhythm of your Inner Urge—your total birth vibration.

CHAPTER XIX
WHAT DOES THE FUTURE HOLD?

YOUR present earth experience will always be colored by the total digit of your birth, yet within this large span your life moves in cycles of greater or less degree from beginning to infinity. Each year brings certain influences to bear upon you and your environment which it would be well to note if you desire to prosper. Regulating your activities in accord with the year's vibrations eliminates cross-currents and establishes you harmoniously with the universal stream of progress.

27-Year Cycles

Your life is divided into three large periods, governed by the digits of your birth path, during which time you should cultivate the qualities and engage in the activities which such vibration indicates.

The digit of your month controls from 1 through 27 years of age.

The digit of your day governs from 27 through 54.

The digit of your year is the controlling vibration from 54 on.

While the total digit of your birth should always be given paramount consideration, the sooner you learn the lessons of its respective digits, the sooner will you pass from your month into your day and from your day into your year, arriving at your ultimate goal much quicker than if you meekly await your turn at the close of the cycle.

9-Year Cycles

Each letter of your *given names* controls a period of 9 years. When you have passed through these once you return and begin again with the first letter.

Yearly Influences

Within the larger cycles each year brings you its own particular lessons. Among the first to be considered is the general aspect of the year itself, found by adding its digits.

In our first edition, published in 1926, we made the prophecy shown here under 1927. This was before Lindbergh, Chamberlain and Byrd had made their memorable flights across the Atlantic, Lindbergh landing in Paris on May 21st, 1927. We knew, however, that so long as the years maintain their cyclic sway, 1927 would bring pioneer (10) feats of daring in the Air (10).

Every year which adds to 10 marks the beginning of a new era or cycle of events, whether it be in the life of individuals, nations, or in world affairs.

1927 is 1-9-2-7, totalling 19—10 or 1—a splendid year in which to make that contemplated change, promote some new enterprise, place a new invention upon the market or add another line to your present operations. Aviation will receive a new impetus. This is a period in which you must stand firmly on your own feet, discard the advice of others and listen carefully to your own intuition, exercising initiative and aggressiveness at all times. You cannot afford to be lazy in a 1 year; if you are, some one is apt to step on you. Wake up to your real possibilities!

1928 is 1-9-2-8, totaling 20 or 2. This is the time to collect materials, statistics, information—systematize it and build your idea into concrete form, ready for public approval the coming year. Exercise patience and tact in all your dealings. You cannot afford to be angry this year. Develop a hobby, study dramatic art, build, maintain and operate.

The positive aspect of 2—the exercise of diplomacy in the establishment of peace and harmony between existing groups, has already been evidenced in 1928 through the signing of the Kellogg Peace Pact, the Good-Will flight of Col. Lindbergh and the recent trip of President Hoover to the Central and South American States.

The adverse aspect of 2 is death (20) or dissolution and the early part of the year has already witnessed the passing of many famous men.

2 being a diplomatic number is naturally in rhythm with politics. This being a Presidential year recalls to mind the first Republican Convention, held in 1856, also a 20 year.

1929 is 1-9-2-9, totaling 21 or 3. Behold the women, prominent in politics and in all high places! This is the year when the men should plan to take that long deferred vacation. Art, beauty, health and humanitarian programs will be the order of the day. Life will take on a new expression, with the women holding sway.

1930 is 1-9-3-0, totaling 13 or 4. This year will mark substantial building progress in all lines, especially in education, manufacturing and commercial affairs. If you wish to be in harmony with the universal forces you must attune your life to regularity in work, play, living and giving, exercising economy, thrift, discrimination, leaving nothing undone to accomplish your ends. Next year you'll have time to travel.

1931 is 1-9-3-1, totaling 14 or 5. This year will see relief from the strenuosity of 1930. You may spend your summer in the Rockies and winter in Florida if you stayed on the job last year. But before you go, be sure your affairs are in perfect order, as all people, policies and programs will be subject to investigation. All hidden corners will be thoroughly searched and detectives will find their business thriving. Psychology, metaphysics, vocational guidance, will be popular subjects of discussion, while "How to stay forever young" will be the paramount theme of the day. This is the time to investigate your prospects among the opposite sex, as next year you may want to settle down.

1932 is 1-9-3-2, totaling 15 or 6. A splendid year to invest in a wedding ring, build a home and establish your self in domesticity. Business will be active, with educational and health programs prominent in the daily press. It is a period in which you must assume responsibility graciously if you wish to grow. And don't forget to smile, whether you feel like it or not, for the blues are taboo in 1932.

1933 is 1-9-3-3, totaling 16 or 7. Now is the time to enter the field of finance, go into business for yourself, or hie yourself to the country and engage in agriculture. Take things easy as much as you can, reserving some time each day for quiet meditation, allowing your intuition to lead the way. Bring everything you do to ultimate perfection, keep every engagement on the dot, talk little, think much, and you will be able to "cash in" on your ideas in 1934.

1934 is 1-9-3-4, totaling 17 or 8—a year of prosperity, marked by forward strides in business and commercial activities, with engineering feats that startle the world. Use reason, tact and good judgment in all your affairs, keeping a perfect balance between earth and the higher realm.

Similar influences apply to the months within each year, according to their numerical order in the calendar.

1910 was the last 11 year and there will not be another until 2009, but in the month of November of every year the 11 influence will be apparent in spiritualistic and psychic phenomena, while matters of religion will be widely discussed. It is a splendid month for promotion schemes and the spread of new propaganda.

1939 is the next 22 year. This should be marked by the largest humanitarian projects which the world has ever known. Pure materialism will give way to more spiritual things, while the dreamers will become practical doers. It will be a pivotal year of great import in the history of the twentieth century.

In 1858, an outstanding 22 year in the last century, the first trans-Atlantic cable was laid, cementing nations and large interests as no previous achievement had ever done. What 1939 holds in store, we can scarce conjecture!

Your Lessons This Year

Your most important influence for any year is found by adding the digits of your month and day to the digit of such year.

Lindbergh was born February 4, 1902. Thus his dominant influence for 1927, when he made his epic flight was 7—(Feb. 4, 1927 is 2+4+10=16=7).

Whenever your influence for the year is 7 you should bring your affairs to a high state of perfection and completion. You should stand alone, act on your intuition and not allow others to swerve you from the path of your chief ambition. It is a time when you should gain recognition for previous efforts made.

Col. Lindbergh's influence for 1928 is 2+4+2 or 8, business organization and executive duties, upon which he has already entered.

A yearly influence of 9 always marks the closing of a large cycle in some way, perhaps a long journey, but in 10 you must make a decision, stand boldly on your own feet and expect assistance from no one. If you do not move on, into a new environment of some kind, or put a new idea into operation, of your own free will, circumstances often step in and force the situation.

Cycles in National Events

Nations as well as individuals move in cycles, while the nature of important events is always significantly shown in the date vibration.

Independence Day, July 4, 1776 (7-4-3), an 11-3 day, marked the birth of a new government, or a new era of self-expression of far-reaching influence.

The first strong note in our existence as an individual nation was struck on October 19, 1781, (10+10+8=10) a 1 day, when at Yorktown the Colonies gained their decisive victory over the British and brought to an end the Revolutionary War. The three 1s in this date throw their firm positive force in the direction of the 8, the highest physical number, showing not only the birth of the strongest nation (1) on earth, but one bound to be a promoter (1) of big business (8) throughout the world, co-operating (8) with other nations, yet always maintaining its distinctive individuality and independent (1) atmosphere.

The most important event of the present generation occurred November 11, 1918, at 11 o'clock a. m., when the Armistice was signed. 11 always stands for a new beginning and in this particular date, the complete triangle of 11s, in a year which totals 10 (11-11-11-10), shows not only the entrance of a new era, but also one of universal import, which will be marked by the most dynamic, unusual and psychic influences which the world has yet known.

It is interesting to note that the elections for President (11) of the United States (4) are held every 4 years—the vibration of its Day and Name. Occurring in November, an 11 month, followed by inauguration in March, a 3 month, they bring the 3 outstanding vibrations of the Birth-date into play—11-3 and 4.

The United States is now 152 years old, in the 8th year of its 13th cycle of 12 which closes 4 years hence. It is also in its 22nd cycle of 7 which ends in 1930. Between 1930 and 1932 when these two closing influences converge, there is apt to be an unusual amount of nervous tension in all phases of life, but having weathered the temporary confusion, 1933 should see a new era of economic adjustment and bring a brighter day in the world's affairs.

CHAPTER XX

THE U. S. A. AND THE 5 VIBRATION

Your destiny is linked with the country in which you live. The very atmosphere is permeated with the dominant vibrations, hopes and desires which gave it birth.

How the great law of vibration operates to control the destinies of nations and individuals, producing leaders who really represent the desires of the people and who are in harmony with the country itself, is revealed by the number vibrations of the U. S. A. and a few of its Presidents.

```
                        U.  S.  A.
                        3   1   1
                        ─────────
                            5

        8
       ──
       17                6      = 14 = (5)—Soul—
      3 9 5             1 5            desire.
     U N I T E D     S T A T E S
      5 2   4       1 2   2   1
      ──────────    ─────────
          11            6      = (11-6)—Body—
                                      personality.
     3 5 9 2 5 4   1 2 1 2 5 1
        28              12
        ──              ──
         1       +       3      = (4)—Destiny.

Birth date:   July 4    1776
              7   4      21
              ──         ──
              11          3     = (11-3)—Spirit—
                                        work.
          7          = (7)—Soul—desire.
         ──
         10
     ──────────────────────
      1     5     9       1
      A  M  E  R  I  C  A
     4     9           3
     ─────────────────
         16
         ──
          7          = (7)—Body—personality.
     1 4 5 9 9 3 1
        32
        ──
         5           = 5—Destiny.
```

(139)

When the pioneers of this country decided to form a government of their own they plainly showed their desire for freedom of thought and action in the name they chose, the vowels of which total 5. Their faith in this particular continent as the fruition of their dreams is found in the total of America, 5, while the abbreviation of the whole name to U. S. A. further accentuates its life-giving qualities and the varied opportunities within its borders.

The Declaration of Independence was signed on July 4th, 1776, an 11-3 day. In earlier chapters we found that 3 stands for complete expression, 1 representing the father, 2 the mother and 3 the child, while 11 is a universal number. The joint vibration of 11-3 shows the birth of a new country, a child on the high plane of 11, one who has come to be an inspirational leader in the promotion of the highest ideals and a joy-bringer to all the world in lines of human betterment.

The strong personality vibration of 11-6 shows this to be a country of big business, large educational and health projects, with the home idea enlarged to include many philanthropic institutions.

The 4 destiny made up of 1 and 3 shows strength and substantiality. Through the exercise of economy and thrift, through the promotion of education and the development of individual self-expression among its citizens, it has laid the cornerstone of an enduring civilization upon which future generations can build with safety.

The Spirit of its birth path of 11-3 (5 in its lesser aspect) is shown in the *Declaration of Independence* (3-3-8 totaling 14 or 5); its rejuvenating, life (5) giving power (5) lies in the beacon light (11) of freedom (3) with which it illumines the world.

Presidents Representative of the U. S. A.

Out of 29 occupants of the President (11)s chair, 28 of them have had, either in their name or birth date, those vibrations which indicate true leadership ability—10, 11 or 22. In addition to this dynamic quality, those who seem to have sensed most keenly the true pulse of the people have had the 5 vibration in a strong aspect. This gave them an understanding, not only of the nation's ideals but of the methods to pursue in carrying out the work which this country came to do.

George Washington with a vowel of $7+7=14=(5)$ was the pioneer *Spirit* who sought to implant the ideal of freedom and life (5) into the hearts of his people.

Abraham Lincoln, born February 12, 1809 ($2+3+9=14=5$) who came with a 5 *work* to accomplish, strove to establish this ideal in reality in the economic and personal *life* of the nation.

Woodrow Wilson, with a Destiny of 22-5-11 (his original name being Thomas Woodrow Wilson), represented the *intellectual* concept of this ideal in its universal aspect, which he sought to make real through the League of Nations.

In these three, as expressed in *The Unfinished Work of the United States* by C. De Vos, we find a vivid picture of the spirit, life and intelligence of the United States of America.

Another forceful leader was Theodore Roosevelt, who with his strong diplomatic 22-5 vibration, sought to cement a greater friendship with other countries, while Calvin Coolidge with a 5 Personality (consonants) and 5 Name worked to *carry on,* the task left unfinished by his predecessors.

CHAPTER XXI
NUMBERS TELL THE TRUTH
Illustrious Examples

THE most convincing proof of the truth of numbers is found by a visit to the halls of fame. A few examples will serve to show the accurate correspondence between the individual's life achievement and the dominant vibrations in his name.

Abraham Lincoln (1)

"LET us have faith that right makes might; and in that faith let us to the end dare to do our duty as we understand it."

					Usual Signature	
	3	+	6	= 9	1 + 6	=7
Vowels:	1 1 1		9 6		1 9 6	
	ABRAHAM	L I NCOLN		A.	L I NCOLN	
Consonants:	2 9 8 4	3 5 3 3 5		3	5 3 3 5	
	23	19			19	
	5	+	13	= 6	10 =	10
Total name:	8	+	7 =15= 6	1 + 7 =		8

Born February 12, 1809
18
2 + 3 + 9=14= 5 —Birth patn.

Abraham Lincoln is the personification of the courageous, fearless "do and dare" spirit of the 3 "A"s of his first name and the 10 personality of Lincoln. A born leader, with the indomitable persistence of the true pioneer, his strong and striking individuality mingled with the crowd yet always remained as one apart. With a big heart (9) and a sensitive soul (7) he was able to get the viewpoint (1) of those about him, yet when it came to a crucial situation he discarded their advice and relied upon his

Illustrious Examples

ABRAHAM LINCOLN
(1),

JANE ADDAMS
(6)

RING W. LARDNER
(3)

MARY PICKFORD
(4)

God and his own intuition—the only path for a true 1 to follow if he desires success.

The 8 of Abraham and of "A. Lincoln" both show his large executive driving force, coupled with keen discrimination, tact and judgment. The 6 personality reveals his great interest in education and his conscientious sense of duty toward home and country. The vowel trinity of 3-6-9 not only gave him talent for law, but also the power to express his ideas with beauty and strength, in a clear, convincing manner.

His birth path of 5 shows that he came to work with humanity, to espouse the cause of freedom, to exercise power, and that in the legal profession (3 or 9) he would be most apt to find that outlet for free expression which his soul desired and which should eventually lead to his life work.

That he learned his lesson well and splendidly fulfilled his destiny—6, the fearless assumption of large responsibilities—none doubt. His soul has gone on, yet whenever his *name* is mentioned the principles for which he stood are again broadcast to the universe by our own thought vibrations. Thus does his powerful influence still remain, through his *name*, to follow him forever.

The 2 Vibration

THE different editions of "Who's Who in America" are replete with Hannas who have been prominent in that special field of the 2 vibration, diplomacy. One of the most famous was the late Senator Marcus Alonzo (Mark) Hanna, who played such an important part in the political history of the United States during the days of President McKinley.

```
              2        — 2
        1          1
     H  A  N  N  A
     8     5  5
        ─────
          18          —9
     8  1  5  5  1
        ─────
          2∅          —2
```

More recent figures of note are:

Hugh Henry Hanna, publicist, active in currency reform legislation, appointed by President Roosevelt in 1903 as chairman of the Commission on International Exchange.

Hugh Sisson Hanna, economist, whose 2 talent for statistics brought him into public recognition through his services with the United States Bureau of Labor Statistics, 1908-1918, and gained for him the position of Chief Examiner of the National War Labor Board in 1918-19. As an author his writings have dealt with accidents and their prevention, wages, labor laws and matters of finance.

Philip C. Hanna, recently retired Consul-General, active in foreign service, influential in preserving friendly relations with Mexico during the revolution in that country in 1914, now a lecturer on Latin American and international subjects.

Matthew Elting Hanna, present member of the diplomatic service at Washington, representative of the United States at German imperial maneuvers in 1911, with the American Embassy at Mexico from 1917 to 1921, since which time he has been in charge of Mexican affairs in the Department of State.

Ring W. Lardner (3)

A WONDERFUL exponent of the *humor* of 3 is found in Ring W. Lardner, one of the most popular joy-bringers (3) of the day.

```
                9      +       6     = 15 =(6)
.Vowels:        9              1    5              Without the "W"
              R I NG  W.  LARDNER                 Vowels — 6
Consonants: 9   5 7   5   3  9 4 5   9            Cons. — 6
              21                30                 Total — 3
              3 + 5      +      3     =(11)
Total name: 9 9 5 7   5   3 1 9 4 5 5 9
              30                36
              3 + 5      +      9     =17=(8)
               Born   March   6,  1885
                      3  +  6 + 22    =(9-22)—Birth path
```

With the total digit of 3 appearing four times in his name and again in his birth, how can this gentleman help being funny?

The complete trinity of literary expression, 3-6-9, is also found in both name and birth path, the latter total of 9-22 showing that he has come to be an outstanding figure in his line, bringing home to his readers, through his humor and imagination, the practical side of life in mirth-coated pills.

The 11 personality shows a winning vibration when it comes to making a striking, likable, dynamic impression upon other people. Even if we leave out the "W," which is frequently done, we still have a total of 6—one who can give splendid advice to the other fellow. This signature makes the vowels and consonants even, giving him absolute poise, with a good balance of sense and non-sense in the expression (3) of his art (3).

If anyone ever found his "right pew" it would seem that Mr. Lardner has, yet we would say that he has still larger worlds to conquer. His birth path of 9-22 shows that he has come, not only to cheer the world upon its way, but to take an active part in national affairs and in diplomatic circles.

Illustrious Examples

THEODORE ROOSEVELT
(22 and 5)

WOODROW WILSON
(5 and 11)

HENRY FORD
(7)

CALVIN COOLIDGE
(7)

Mary Pickford (4)

M ARY PICKFORD, one of the most loved film stars, is a splendid example of the wonderful achievement which can be made with the substantial 4 vibration.

$$8 \quad + \quad \frac{6}{15} \quad =14= (5)$$

Vowels:
$$\begin{array}{cc} 1 \quad 7 & 9 \qquad 6 \\ \text{M A R Y} & \text{P I C K F O R D} \end{array}$$

Consonants:
$$\begin{array}{cc} 4 \quad 9 & 7 \quad 3\ 2\ 6 \quad 9\ 4 \\ \hline \frac{13}{4} & \frac{31}{4} \end{array}$$

Total name:
$$\begin{array}{cc} 4\ 1\ 9\ 7 & 7\ 9\ 3\ 2\ 6\ 6\ 9\ 4 \\ \frac{21}{3} \quad + & \frac{46}{1\emptyset} \end{array} = (8)$$

$$=(4)$$

Born April 8, 1893
$$4 + 8 + \frac{\overline{21}}{3} = 15 = (6) — \text{Birth path.}$$

The general interpretation of number 4 is hard work and limitation, but when composed of 3 and 1, the positive, creative 1 accentuates the 3 powers of artistic expression and makes the individual a keen intellectual builder (4) along lines of art (3) in no uncertain measure.

The 8 consonants show a strong personality, radiating an atmosphere of health, success and prosperity. The 5 vowels give an intense love of life from every angle with the ability to inject spice into all her activities. The 10 of Pickford not only bestows leadership qualities, but also a distinctive individuality, making her unique in her field.

She has been a most efficient (4) joy-bringer (3), putting the originality of 1 and the youth of 5 into the artistic expression (3) of those things which make the multitude happy. Her executive ability, good judgment and sense of values, evidenced by the two 8s and three 4s in her name, account for her success in business.

The lesson of her 6 birth path,—happy expression in service for others,—made up of 4-8-3, shows that the artistic talent of 3 and 6 will naturally fall in the field of imitation (4 and 8)—dramatic art.

It is significant to note that Mary Pickford made her reputation on the screen during the period of her life controlled by the 4 of her month (1-27) and that the name she chose carried the same vibration.

Jackie Coogan, the most famous boy star of the day, is also a 4, made up of 3 and 1. So, you who have the 4 vibration, cheer up! You may have to work, but if you are happy in doing it, and successful in bringing joy to others, you will likewise arrive—either at Hollywood or some place better.

Woodrow Wilson (5 and 11)

MANY are the Presidents of the United States who have predominated in the 5 vibration, answering the desire of the "United States" shown in its 5 vowels. A recent figure in the cause of universal freedom and lasting peace was the late Woodrow Wilson.

```
                          9        +     6      =15=(6)
Vowels:            6 6       6          9    6
                   W O O D R O W    W I L S O N
Consonants:  5         4 9       5    5   3 1     5
                          5        +     5      =10= (1)
Total:       5 6 6 4 9 6 5    5 9 3 1 6 5
                     41                  29
                      5        +        11      = (5-11)
             Born  December  28,   1856
                     12        10       20
                      3   +    1   +     2 =(6)—Birth date.
Higher aspect of path—12       10
                              22       +   2 =(22-2)
```

5 appears four times in the above digit totals and in addition thereto is the first letter of both names, casting its broad humanitarian influence over the educational "O"s and total 6 vowels.

President Wilson's original name, Thomas Woodrow Wilson, with its 22 vowels and total of 22-5-11, certainly proclaimed a master soul whose destiny it was to project his high ideals into the heart of the universe.

As a historian (5Ø), his writings are colored by the freedom and humanity aspect of the 5 vibration—"George Washington," "A History of the American People," "Free Life," "The New Freedom," "When a Man Comes to Himself," "On Being Human," and many others of like character.

With a 6 birth vibration, as a college professor he was in his right vocation, which, when successfully mastered, led him into his larger destiny, teaching the higher truths to all mankind. Right here, however, we desire to call attention to the higher aspect of his birth path, revealed by the double numbers. December is the 12th month. Adding the month to the 10 day before reducing, we have 22, which with the 2 year makes his total vibration 22-2. Both 22 and 2 are diplomats and peacemakers, students of the laws of cause and effect, linking the spiritual with the material and striving to strike an even balance. As a university professor President Wilson was a splendid 6, but as a world leader (22) in the promotion of peace (2) he reached the heights of his higher calling.

Although he did not live to see realized the humanitarian principles for which he strove so mightily, his efforts were not lost. The strong positive thought currents of peace

Illustrious Examples

COLONEL GOETHALS
(8)

MAUDE ADAMS
(8)

IRVIN S. COBB
(9)

COL. CHAS. A. LINDBERGH
(11)

which he injected into the atmosphere have been gathering momentum ever since.

Theodore Roosevelt (22 and 5)

O NE of the most powerful men of recent years, as well as one of the most popular, was Theodore Roosevelt, a typical 5, dominated by the 22 vibration.

```
                   22        +         22          =(22-22)
Vowels:          5 6  6   5       6 6  5   5
               T H E O D O R E   R O O S E V E L T
Consonants: 2 8      4   9       9    1    4   3 2
                     5        +        1Ø           =(6)
Total:      2 8 5  6 4  6 9 5   9 6 6 1 5  4 5 3 2
                    45                 4 1
                     9        +         5           =14=(5)
            Born October  27,  1858
                 1Ø  +  9 = 22       =(1Ø-22)—Birth path.
```

A born leader, diplomat and executive, Theodore Roosevelt brought his large 22 ideas into practical use for the benefit of the many. His fearlessness (1) and great personal magnetism, evidenced by the many 5s, gave him a wonderful influence over others, which his natural tact and diplomacy turned into constructive channels.

A lover of life from every angle, happy in world travel, he ran true to form even in sport as the greatest (22) hunter (5) of his day.

His contributions to American literature reveal the fluency of speech and the big heart of his 9 vibration, while the 6 personality shows his strong love for home and family.

Well did he learn his lesson of 1-22 and become an outstanding (1) figure in world affairs (22), a diplomat among diplomats, popular among foreign kings and queens as well as in his own country.

Jane Addams (6)

THE pioneer home-maker among the women of the world is Jane Addams, founder of Hull House, in the city of Chicago.

```
                      6    +    2                    =(8)
Vowels:            1     5    1            1
                 J A   N  E   A  D  D  A  M  S
Consonants:      1     5        4  4     4  1
                      6    +              4          =(10)
Total:           1 1  5  5   1  4  4  1  4  1
                      12                 15
                       3   +              6          =(9)
             Born  September  6,    1860
                                     15
                    9   +   6  +  6  =21=(3)
```

The 6 vibration, of home, education and happy service to others, appears three times in the digits of the above name and twice in the birth path, while the strong positive force of the five 1's gives added power and authority to this illustrious woman who has established a world model community center where home-building is taught from every angle.

The complete trinity of balanced expression on the high plane is shown in her total digits of 8-9-10, the 8 giving her executive ability, diplomacy, tact, driving qualities; the 10, originality and the strength to stand her own ground despite public opinion or adverse circumstances; the 9, the ability to express her ideas in a large humanitarian way, with sympathy and understanding. The full name also contains the trinity of artistic and literary expression, 3-6-9, enabling her to combine the esthetic side of life with the practicality of her many 4's.

As a peace envoy, visiting the governments of the world

in the interest of peace, she represented the mothers of all time in their united prayer that wars shall cease.

Calvin Coolidge (7) — Henry Ford (7)

TWO noteworthy individuals whose total names are both 7-7=14=5 and whose birthdays fall in the 7th month.

$$\frac{1\emptyset}{\underset{CALVIN}{1\quad 9}} + \frac{8}{\underset{COOLIDGE}{6\ 6\quad 9\quad 5}} = (9) \qquad \frac{3}{\underset{HENRY}{5\quad 7}} + \frac{6}{\underset{FORD}{6}} = (9)$$

$$\begin{array}{cc} 3\ 34\ 5\ 3 & 3\ 47 \\ \hline 6 & + \quad 8 \quad =14=(5) \end{array} \qquad \begin{array}{cc} 8\ \ 59 & 6\ \ 94 \\ \hline 22 & 1\emptyset \quad =(22\text{-}1) \end{array}$$

$$\frac{3\ 1\ 3\ 4\ 9\ 5}{\underset{7}{25}} + \frac{3\ 6\ 6\ 3\ 9\ 4\ 7\ 5}{\underset{7}{43}} =14=(5) \qquad \frac{8\ 5\ 5\ 9\ 7}{\underset{7}{34}} + \frac{6\ 9\ 9\ 4}{\underset{7}{25}} = 4 = (5)$$

$$\text{Born July } \frac{4,}{7}\ \ \frac{1872}{\underset{4}{18}}$$
$$\frac{11}{} + \frac{9}{} = (11\text{-}9)$$

$$\text{Born July 30, } \frac{1863}{18}$$
$$7 + 3 + 9 = 19 = (1\emptyset)$$

Both of these men, supreme in their realm, typify the strength, firmness, solidarity and large achievement of the true 7 vibration. They rely on their own intuition and keep well their own counsel, directing the activities of others with confidence and poise.

5 is usually considered a changeable number, but the unusual power which rests in the hands of these two men is due to the stabilizing force of the two 7s, which brings continuity of thought, will power, perfection of detail and thoroughness of execution into every project. 5 always denotes an investigative mind and brings many interesting experiences to pass in the life of the individual, but when made up of 7 plus 7 it is a vibration of unusual accomplish-

ment, combining intuition with wisdom and an instinctive understanding of human nature with the power to rule.

Another illustrious example is found in George Washington, whose destiny (full name) was 7 and whose vowels had the magic vibration of 7-7=14=5.

Maude Adams (8)—Colonel Goethals (8)

THE two widely divergent aspects of the 8 vibration are aptly shown in the celebrated actress of Peter Pan fame and the noted engineer who brought to completion the great Panama Canal.

```
          9        +      2          = (11)
       1  3   5        1     1
       M  A  U  D  E   A  D  A  M  S
       4     4         4     4  1
          8        +         9      =17=(8)
     4  1  3  4  5   1  4  1  4  1
          17              11
          8        +       11       =(8-11)
     Born November 11, 1872
                       18
         11      11    9=(11-11-9)
```

```
        7       +     7        +     3       =17=(8)
     5 6   5       1  9   0       6 5   1
     GEORGE     WASHINGTON     GOETHALS
```

```
          8        +        3         =(11)
     6   6   5        6 5     1
     C  O  L  O  N  E  L   G  O  E  T  H  A  L  S
     3  3  5  3        7     2 8   3 1
          5        +         3        = (8)
   3  6  3  6  5  5  3   7  6  5  2  8  1  3  1
          31                 33
          4        +         6        =(1∅)
       Born June 29, 1858
          6    11    22        = (6-11-22)
```

Maude Adams certainly has all the vibrations which could be desired to attract unusual renown. Her vowels give natural inspiration (11) in the line of dramatic (2) art (9) while her birth path of 11-11-9 shows that she has come to gain universal (11) fame in her chosen vocation.

The mere sound of her name creates the impression that here is an individual with a strong 8 personality, executive ability and tact,. who radiates the prosperity atmosphere, while the total 8 of Maude and in her full signature gives marked success, not only in the field of imitation, but also in business and financial avenues as well. Wisely did she choose when she took this powerful nom de plume through which to gain outstanding (11) success in dramatic (8) art (9).

Colonel Goethals' talent in engineering (8) is found in the vowels of his original name, while the two 7s help to make his work a model of perfection and completion. The name whose vibration he has carried for many years reveals a strong executive, forceful 8 personality, while his 11 vowel total throws its leadership qualities over the 8 of Colonel, giving him driving force and unusual engineering ability. This he also turned to good account in solving the large health (3) problems which confronted him at every turn in the Canal Zone.

His high birth vibrations show that he came to render a humanitarian service (6) of universal magnitude (11 and 22). 22 is a diplomatic executive, one who brings peace and harmony between opposing factions. In building (8) the Panama Canal Colonel Goethals joined two great oceans, resulting in an increase of business, commerce and friendly relations between all peoples.

Irvin S. Cobb (9)

I RVIN S. COBB, whose first name shows the 9 vibration in three aspects, is a wonderful example of the 9 literary genius who travels the globe in search of new adventures with which to punctuate his fluent expression.

$$
\begin{array}{cccccc}
9 & & + & & 6 & =15=(6) \\
\hline
9 \qquad 9 & & & & \overline{6} & \\
\text{I R V I N} & \text{S.} & & \text{C O B B} & & \\
9\ 4 \quad 5 & 1 & & 3\ \ ?\ \ 2 & & \\
\hline
9 & + & 1 & + & \iota & =17=(8) \\
9\ 9\ 4\ 9\ 5 & 1 & & 3\ 6\ 2\ 2 & & \\
\hline
36 & & & 13 & & \\
\hline
9 & + & 1 & + & \overline{4} & =14=(5)
\end{array}
$$

Born June 23, 1876
6   5   22
─────────────
11   =(11-22)—Birth path.

A genial, whole-souled fellow, with large humanitarian ideas, interested in world affairs, is this noted American humorist. Every vibration is present in his name, showing his ability to contact the minds of all classes.

9 being 3×3, gives him abundant humor and sympathetic understanding of human nature, while the 5 makes him an eternal investigator, putting the exuberance of youth into all of his activities. The 1 of "S" adds strength and originality to his splendid building (4) power in the artistic (9) handling of words.

His birth path shows that he has come to render a large (11-22) joy-bringing service (6) to humanity (5) and that especially between the ages of 27 and 54 will his life be filled with varied experiences and much travel (5). His reputation has already encircled the globe, yet we venture to say that after 54, when he comes into the 22 vibration of his year, he will take a more prominent part in world affairs than ever before. Then may he speak, not only with a mirth-provoking humor, but with the power, force and far-reaching influence of a true diplomat.

CHARLES A. LINDBERGH (11)

A radiant light (11) in this Aquarian Age is Col. Charles A. Lindbergh, a true son of Aquarius, Lord of the Air, of the eleventh zodiacal sign. His "solo flight which intrigued the world" has been in truth an *inspirational new beginning* (11) for all mankind—a fitting example for the true 11 who, caring naught for precedent, allows the intuitive (11) voice to lead the way and guide him alone o'er pathless seas to the ultimate goal of his inner vision.

```
        6              1              5        =12—(3)
                      10             14         Soul
     1   5     1 3   3     3      9     5
    C h  a r l e s  A u g u s t u s  L i n d b e r g h
    3 8  9 3  1      7  1 2    1   3  5 4 2   9 7 8
      24-6            11               38-11    =(6=11-
                                                 11)-Body
    3 8 1 9 3 5 1   1 3 7 3 1 2 3 1   3 9 5 4 2 5 9 7 8
        30               21               52
        3                3                7        =13—(4)
                                                   Mind—
                                                   Destiny

        Born February 4:   1902
                           12
          2     4           3 = (9)—Spirit—Inner Urge—Work

      6       5      =(11)      6   1   5    =12—(3)
    Charles Lindbergh         Charles A. Lindbergh
      6       11     =(6-11)    6       11    =(6-11)
      3       7      =(10)      3   1   7     (11)
```

In full name and later signatures, Col. Lindbergh has the 11 vibration of independent leadership in strong aspect. It not only accounts for the dare-devil spirit manifested in his early feats of flying, for his urge to accomplish the

hitherto impossible, but for that instinctive knowing which
enables him to anticipate the question and say just the right
thing at the proper time.   No matter where he goes, his
l u c k goes with him.

$$\frac{3\,3\,3\,2}{11}$$

As 11 is also an emblem of l i g h t, it is interesting to

$$\frac{3\,9\,7\,8\,2}{29\text{-}11}$$

note that the numbers indicating Col. Lindbergh's physical
type (consonants of 6-11-11) are a striking proof of the
findings of Dr. Doonan of Garden City, New York who
examined the flyer just before his flight to Paris, i.e. that
he possessed nearly double perfect vision and that his chest
expansion was 1¾" more than the normal chest expansion
of pugilists.   These unusual physical assets, plus the endurance of his 7 surname, have aided immeasurably in the
realization of his dreams.

From the standpoint of heredity, Col. Lindbergh came
with a wonderful heritage, his surname containing the complete trinity of scientific achievement, 11-5-7. The 11 and
5 gave him inspiration, daring and an interest in research
and investigation, while the 7 brought physical endurance,
stick-to-it-iveness, independence, will-power, a desire to be
alone, and that self-assurance or faith in his own ability
which gave him the power to achieve.   His original low
vowel of 3 accounts for his natural modesty, while the 4
intellect shows a keen analytical mind, splendid mental control, and that 4-square principle of sincerity which has
characterized all his actions.

Charles Lindbergh has an 11 in both vowels and consonants, with the pioneer 10 as a total. After the advertising

(11) which this feat gave him, it was Charles *A*. Lindbergh (11) who adorned the front page, the 11 consonant and 11 *total* indicating a larger outlet and greater opportunity for leadership expression. He had gained the publicity (9) due a birth path of 9 who falls into line with a world (9) program.

The outstanding events of his life have occurred on days having the same vibration as his date of birth, showing the harmony of his actions with his inner urge.

He landed in New York at the end of his cross-country flight, May 12, 1927 (5+3+10=9), a 9 day; completed the first non-stop trans-Atlantic flight from America to Europe on May 21, 1927 (5+3+10=9), also a 9 day, covering the 3600 (9) miles in 33(6) hours, 29(11) minutes and 30(3) seconds, registering from a vibratory standpoint, a time record of 11-9.

Col. Lindbergh types the mastery (11) of the fearless 11, one "whose deeds merit comemmoration among the most notable contributions of American genius to human progress."

HERBERT HOOVER (11)

In a discussion of the Presidential candidates appearing in Character Reading Magazine prior to election, the author stated, "The weight of evidence already in view, indicates that numerically speaking, Herbert Hoover will be our next President."

Vowels   11
                 10   1   8   —(11-8)—Soul—Talents
            Herbert Clark Hoover
Consonants   3   8   3 —(11-3)—Body—Personality
Total Name   4   9   11 —(4-11)—Mind—Destiny
    Birth Date August 10, 1874
             8   10   20 (20)—Spirit—Inner Urge.

Note: We hold 10 a 10 and do not cross off the cipher.

Mr. Hoover with a Destiny of 4-11 and an 11 in five positions, showing mastery (11) on all planes, is ably fitted to serve as President (11) of the United Statees (4).

As a leader in politics (4), his many high vibrations give him the vision, understanding and able (11) judgment (4) to handle the immense problems of this country and carry out its Birth Path Urge of 11-3 for greater humanitarian (3) progress. July 4, 1776 is 7-4-3 or 11-3. As Secretary of Commerce he has already instituted many efficient measures in our industrial program.

His many 11's make him inwardly sensitive, with high ideals and an interest in the spiritual side of life, while the even numbers lend practically to his make-up and establish a definite mould of strength and power for his many inspirational ideas.

Energy (11), action (8), an excellent memory (8), tact (8) and diplomacy (8), with innate engineering (8) ability, enable him to bring his immense projects to a successful conclusion.

Balanced physically, mentally and spiritually, a leader on all planes, he combines reason and logic with keen intuition, quick decision, and that foresight which prepares him for any emergency and makes him master of the situation.

RICHARD EVELYN BYRD (22)

A "Scientific Blazer of Trails"—explorer, hero and Virginia gentleman, is Commander Richard E. Byrd, the first man to fly across the north pole, who a year later with three companions spanned the Atlantic, who has been cited for heroism or extraordinary valor no less than 21 times, and whose present plans to cross the South Pole make him worthy of the honor for the 22nd time.

```
                      8
         10          17                    =25—(7)
        9   1       5  5  7        7
       R i c h a r d   E v e l y n   B y r d
       9  38   94     4  3  5     2  9 4
          33            12           15
           6            3            6   =15—(6)

       9 9 3 8 1 9 4   5 4 5 3 7 5   2 7 9 4
          43             29
           7             11           22   =(7-11-22)
```

Born October 25: 1888
                    25
        10   7   7=24—(6)

His mother says that he was born an adventurer and explorer, absolutely without fear. In 1901 when 12 years old he set out alone on a trip around the world, going first to Manila where a friend of his father was U. S. Circuit Judge, then taking a British tramp schooner to Japan, Ceylon, India and other places. This aroused in him an early interest in sea navigation. On returning home he entered a military academy and later attended Annapolis. He became Lieutenant Commander in 1922.

He is a delicate instrument physically, with his original 6 consonant and later one of 3 as compared with the strong 11s of Lindbergh but this factor is balanced by his unusual mental control (7-11-22), cool head, clear thinking, and intuitive mastery over every situation.

A born leader, working in a co-operative, masterly, diplomatic way, his 22 surname bespeaks his descent from an illustrious family, who for generations back have been men of authority and large affairs, active in the interests of their country.

While the 7 and 11 give him independence of action, stick-to-it-iveness and quick decision, his 22 makes him a keen analyst, working through groups or organizations. On his trip to the South Pole he took down and brought back with him about ten 'ologists—biologists, zoologists, ornithologists, meterologists, etc., as well as experts to study the magnetic forces around the pole.

The inventive genius of his 10 month has found expression in the instruments he has devised for use in aviation, such as the bubble-sextant, sun-compass, drift-indicator and others.

As an organizer (6) of one pioneer (10) movement after another for gaining mastery (11) over nature (7), by air (10) and sea (7), Commander Byrd has contributed invaluable scientific (7) knowledge (6) to our present civilization.

He has not only carried out the dictates of his inner urge (10-7-7-6), toward the fulfillment of his destiny (7-11-22), but in a still larger way reflects the qualities of the 22 who seeks to correlate the spiritual with the material and bring peace to all mankind. In an interview published in the Literary Digest in July, 1927, on being asked what he was thinking about when he crossed the pole, he replied in part,

"It is not the geographical but the moral limitations of the world that must be charted and the really great explorers will be those who find the way to universal reconstruction, the first step in which is the abolition of war and the needless destruction of human life."

A fearless, indomitable soul, possessed of logic, intuition and large vision, "Dick Byrd" (9-22) who seeks to master

(22) the world (9), combines the perfect type of officer and gentleman with that of the most intrepid explorer of the present day.

Unlike Alexander the Great, may he never have cause to weep because of no more worlds to conquer! Having planted the American flag on the South Pole, 10,000 feet above sea level, may this dauntless Byrd of Passage wing his way to greater heights as a true 22 (diplomatic adjuster between large groups or bodies) and establish communication with the planet Mars.

IN CONCLUSION

MAY health, harmony and success, in large measure, attend the ambitious soul who has read thus far.

To aid you in working out your individual problem, we have appended a list of over 1,500 names with their vowel, consonant and total number values. Remember, however, that, whatever your lesson or name may be, there is power in every number when you conform in truth to its higher nature and attune your life to its dominant note.

May your knowledge of the law prosper you and each day be filled with vibrations of peace, happiness and glorious achievement, is the sincere wish of the author.

> Let naught deter you from your goal,
> But be the master of your soul,
> Knowing well the spoken word
> From the vibrant ether of your world
> Creates the form you hold in mind.
>
> Think not your aim can be too high:
> DESIRE the goal doth prophesy,
> And nothing is impossible;
> For the Law, which stands invincible,
> Returns to you your thoughts in kind.

1,500 Names and Their Number Values

The first number after each name shows its total value; the second number its vowel total, and the third, its consonant total.

Aaron	22—8-5		Adam	10—2-8
Abbe	10—6-4		Adams	11—2-9
Abbie	10—6-4		Addison	3—7-5
Abbot	4—7-6		Adel	4—6-7
Abel	11—6-5		Adela	5—7-7
Aberdeen	9—7-2		Adelaide	5—3-11
Abigail	5—2-3		Adelon	6—3-3
Abihu	5—4-10		Adelphi	10—6-22
Abijah	22—11-11		Adler	22—6-7
Abilene	3—2-10		Adonais	9—8-10
Abner	22—6-7		Adonis	8—7-10
Abraham	8—3-5		Adrian	11—11-9
Abram	8—2-6		Aeneas	9—3-6
Abruzzo	10—10-9		Aeolia	7—22-3
Absalom	9—8-10		Aeschylus	5—7-7
Achates	3—7-5		Aesop	2—3-8
Achilles	6—6-9		Agard	22—2-2
Ackerman	3—7-5		Agatha	2—3-8
Acla	8—2-6		Agnes	10—6-4
Aconcio	6—22-11		Agricola	3—8-22
Acres	10—6-4		Agrippa	5—11-3
Acton	8—7-10		Ahab	3—2-1
Ada	6—2-4		Aida	6—11-4
Adair	6—11-4		Aikin	8—1-7
Adalbert	9—7-2		Ainsworth	10—7-3
Adalia	10—3-7		Aitken	6—6-9
Adaline	10—7-3		Ajax	9—2-7

Alameda - - 10—8-11	Alta - - - - 7—2-5
Alamo - - - 6—8-7	Alton - - 8—7-10
Alba - - - - 7—2-5	Alva - - - - 9—2-7
Albert - - - 22—6-7	Alvarado - - 11—9-2
Alberta - - - 5—7-7	Alvarez - - - 4—7-6
Albina - - - 3—11-10	Amanda - - - 7—3-4
Albinus - - - 6—4-11	Amber - - - 3—6-6
Alcott - - - 8—7-10	Ambrose - - 10—3-7
Alcyone - - - 3—1-11	Amelia - - - 5—7-7
Aldan - - - 5—2-3	America - - - 5—7-7
Alden - - - 9—6-3	Ames - - - 11—6-5
Aldine - - - 9—6-3	Amie - - - 10—6-4
Aldred - - - 8—6-2	Amy - - - - 3—8-4
Aldrich - - 10—10-9	Anabel - - - 8—7-10
Alene - - - 10—11-8	Ananias - - - 5—3-11
Alesia - - - 2—7-4	Anastasia - - 22—4-9
Alexander - - 3—3-9	Andersen - - 8—11-6
Alexandra - - 8—8-9	Anderson - - - 9—3-6
Alexis - - - 7—6-10	Andre - - - 6—6-9
Alfaro - - - 8—8-9	Andrew - - - 11—6-5
Alfonso - - - 10—4-6	Andrews - - - 3—6-6
Alfred - - - 10—6-22	Angel - - - 3—6-6
Alice - - - - 3—6-6	Angelina - - - 9—7-2
Alicia - - - 8—2-6	Angelo - - - 9—3-6
Alise - - - - 10—6-4	Anita - - - 9—11-7
Alla - - - - 8—2-6	Ann - - - 11—1-10
Allan - - - 4—2-11	Anna - - - 3—2-10
Allen - - - 8—6-11	Annabelle - - 3—3-9
Allie - - - - 3—6-6	Anne - - - 7—6-10
Allison - - - 10—7-3	Annie - - - 7—6-10
Alma - - - - 9—2-7	Anson - - - 9—7-11
Alonzo - - - 11—4-7	Anthony - - - 7—5-2

Anton	- - -	10—7-3
Antonio	- - -	7—22-3
Aphrodite	- -	6—3-3
Apollo	- - -	8-4-4
Apollos	- - -	9-4-5
Aquila	- - -	7—5-11
Archer	- - -	8—6-11
Archibald	- -	4—11-11
Arden	- - -	6—6-9
Ariel	- - - -	9—6-3
Arion	- - -	3—7-5
Arles	- - -	10—6-4
Arlo	- - -	10—7-3
Arne	- - - -	2—6-5
Arno	- - - -	3—7-5
Arnold	- - -	10—7-3
Arthur	- - -	5—4-10
Asa	- - - -	3—2-1
Asher	- - - -	6—6-9
Ashland	- - -	5—2-3
Ashton	- - -	5—7-7
Aster	- - - -	9—6-3
Astor	- - -	10—7-3
Atchison	- -	8—7-10
Athalia	- - -	7—3-4
Aubrey	- - -	9-9-9
Auburn	- - -	5—7-7
Audrey	- - -	11—9-2
Auerbach	- -	5—10-4
Augusta	- -	9—8-10
Augustine	- -	9—3-6
Aurelia	- -	4—10-3
Aurelius	- - -	7—3-4
Aurora	- -	11—11-9
Austin	- - -	3—4-8
Ava	- - - -	6—2-4
Avalon	- - -	2—8-3
Avis	- - -	6—10-5
Avon	- - - -	7—7-9
Bab	- - - -	5—1-4
Babbitt	- -	2—10-10
Babcock	- - -	10—7-3
Bach	- - - -	5—1-4
Bacon	- - -	8—7-10
Bain	- - -	8—10-7
Baird	- - -	7—10-6
Baker	- - -	10—6-4
Balbo	- - - -	5—7-7
Baldwin	- -	11—10-10
Balfour	- - -	3—10-2
Ball	- - - -	9—1-8
Ballou	- - -	9—10-8
Balzac	- - -	9—2-7
Bana	- - - -	9—2-7
Bancroft	- - -	7—7-9
Banks	- - -	11—1-10
Bara	- - - -	4—2-11
Barbara	- - -	7—3-22
Barclay	- - -	8—2-6
Bardell	- - -	9—6-3
Barker	- - -	10—6-22
Barlow	- -	8—7—10
Barnabas	- -	22—3-10
Barnaby	- - -	9—9-9

Barnard - - -	4—2-11	Belinda - - - 11—6-5
Barnes - - -	5—6-8	Bell - - - - 4—5-8
Barnett - - -	8—6-2	Bella - - - - 5—6-8
Barnum - - -	6—4-2	Belle - - - 9—10-8
Barodel - - -	3—3-9	Ben - - - - 3—5-7
Baron - - -	5—7-7	Benedict - - 8—10-7
Barr - - - -	3—1-2	Benjamin - - 5—6-8
Barrett - - -	3—6-6	Bennett - - 8—10-7
Barrington - -	10—7-3	Benno - - - 5—11-3
Barron - - -	5—7-7	Benson - - - 6—11-4
Barry - - -	10—8-2	Berlin - - - 6—5-10
Bart - - - -	5—1-4	Bernard - - 8—6-11
Barthold - -	8—7-10	Berne - - - 8—10-7
Bartholomew - -	6—9-6	Bernhardt - - 9—6-3
Bartlett - - -	8—6-2	Berry - - - - 5—3-2
Barton - - -	7—7-9	Bert - - - - 9—5-4
Basil - - -	7—10-6	Bertha - - - 9—6-3
Bassett - - -	5—6-8	Bertini - - - 5—5-9
Bastian - -	3—11-10	Bertram - - - 5—6-8
Bates - - -	11—6-5	Bess - - - - 9—5-4
Bauer - - -	2—9-11	Besse - - - 5—10-4
Baxter - - -	7—6-10	Bethel - - - 7—10-6
Bayard - - -	6—2-22	Betty - - - - 9—3-6
Beall - - - -	5—6-8	Beulah - - - 22—9-4
Beatrice - - -	9—2-7	Beverly - - - 8—8-9
Beatrix - - -	7—6-10	Bianca - - - 3—11-10
Becker - - -	8—10-7	Biglow - - - 5—6-8
Becky - - -	10—3-7	Bill - - - - 8—9-8
Bede - - -	7—10-6	Billings - - - 3—9-3
Bedell - -	22—10-3	Birch - - - 4—9-22
Beecher - - -	10—6-22	Bird - - - - 6—9-6
Birdie - - -	11—5-6	Beethoven - - 6—3-3

Biron - - - -	4—6-7	Brisbane - -	7—6-10
Bismarck - -	4—10-3	Brock - - -	22—6-7
Black - - -	11—1-10	Brooks - - -	8—3-5
Blaine - - -	7—6-10	Bruce - - -	22—8-5
Blair - - -	6—10-5	Bruno - - -	7—9-7
Blake -- - -	4—6-7	Buchanan - -	10—5-5
Blanchard - -	9—2-7	Buck - - -	10—3-7
Blanche - - -	9—6-3	Bunyan - -	5—4-10
Blanco - - -	2—7-4	Burgess - -	10—8-2
Blane - - -	7—6-10	Burke - - - -	3—8-4
Boaz - - -	8—7-10	Burt - - - -	7—3-4
Bob - - - -	10—6-4	Burton - - -	9—9-9
Bobs - - -	11—6-5	Butler - - -	6—8-7
Bonaparte - -	11—4-7	Byron - - -	11—4-7
Bonheur - - -	11—5-6	Cadmus - - -	7—4-3
Bonne - - -	5—11-3	Cadwaller - -	7—7-9
Bonnie - - -	5—2-3	Caesar - - -	2—7-4
Booth - - - -	6—3-3	Cain - - -	9—10-8
Bowles - -	22—11-11	Calve - - -	7—6-10
Boyd - - -	10—4-6	Calvert - - -	9—6-3
Boyle - - - -	5—9-5	Calvin - - -	7—10-6
Bradford - - -	5—7-7	Cameron - - -	6—3-3
Bradshaw - -	4—2-11	Camilla - - -	6—11-4
Bradstreet - -	4—11-11	Campbell - -	10—6-22
Brady - - - -	5—8-6	Cannon - - -	7—7-9
Bragg - - - -	8—1-7	Captain - -	10—11-8
Brand - - -	3—1-2	Carl - - - -	7—1-6
Brewster - -	11—10-10	Carlisle - - -	7—6-10
Brian - - -	8—10-7	Carlos - - -	5—7-7
Brice - - -	10—5-5	Carlyle - - -	4—4-9
Briggs - - -	8—9-8	Carmel - -	7—6-10
Bright - -	10—9-10	Carolina - -	10—8-2

Caroline - - - 5—3-2	Clarence - - 7—11-5
Carolyn - - - 7—5-2	Claribel - - - 8—6-2
Carrie - - - - 9—6-3	Clarice - - - 6—6-9
Carroll - - - 7—7-9	Clarinda - - - 8—11-6
Caruso - - - 5—10-4	Clarissa - - 10—11-8
Carver - - - 4—6-7	Clark - - - 9—1-8
Cary - - - - 2—8-3	Clarke - - - 5—6-8
Casimir - - 9—10-8	Claude - - 10—9-10
Catharine - - - 7—7-9	Claudia - - 6—5-10
Catherine - - 11—2-9	Clayton - - - 9—7-2
Cecil - - - - 5—5-9	Clemens - - 8—10-7
Cecilia - - - 6—6-9	Cleopatra - - 10—4-6
Celeste - - - 6—6-9	Cleveland - - 6—11-22
Celestine - - 11—6-5	Clifford - - 10—6-4
Charles - - - 3—6-6	Clinton - - - 6—6-9
Charlie - - - 11—6-5	Clio - - - - 3—6-6
Charlotte - - - 3—3-9	Clive - - - 6—5-10
Chester - - - 6—10-5	Clyde - - - 22—3-10
Chicago - - - 10—7-3	Clytie - - - 11—3-8
Chloe - - - 7—11-5	Cobb - - - - 4—6-7
Chopin - - - 11—6-5	Cole - - - - 8—11-6
Christian - - 11—10-10	Coleridge - - - 6—7-8
Christiana - - 3—2-10	Coles - - - 9—11-7
Christina - - 11—10-10	Collier - - - 11—2-9
Christine - - 6—5-10	Collins - - - 3—6-6
Christopher - - 4—2-11	Colonel - - - 4—8-5
Christy - - - 3—7-5	Colton - - - 7—3-4
Cicero - - - 8—2-6	Columbus - - 7—3-4
Cinderella - - 11—2-9	Conner - - - 6—11-22
Circe - - - 11—5-6	Conrad - - - 10—7-3
Clara - - - - 8—2-6	Constance - - 4—3-10
Clare - - - - 3-6-6	Conway - - - 9—7-2

Cook - - - -	8—3-5	Daniel - - -	9—6-3
Cooke - - -	22—8-5	Dante - - -	8—6-11
Cooper - - -	9—8-10	Daphne - - -	3—6-6
Cora - - -	10—7-3	Darby - - - -	5—8-6
Corinne - - -	6—2-22	Darcy - - - -	6—8-7
Cornelia - - -	5—3-2	Darius - - -	9—4-5
Cornelius - - -	8—5-3	Darling - -	11—10-10
Cornwall - -	8—7-10	Darwin - - -	6—10-5
Cozzens - - -	9—11-7	David - - -	22—10-3
Crane - - - -	5—6-8	Davies - - -	6—6-9
Crawford - -	7—7-9	Davis - - -	10—10-9
Cristobel - - -	4—2-2	Dean - - - -	6—6-9
Cromwell - -	11—11-9	Deborah - - -	8—3-5
Cullen - - -	22—8-5	Decker - -	10—10-9
Cummins - -	11—3-8	Dee - - - -	5—10-4
Curtis - - - -	9—3-6	Defoe - - -	8—7-10
Curtiss - - -	10—3-7	Delano - - -	6—3-3
Cushing - - -	9—3-6	Delia - - -	22—6-7
Culver - - -	9—8-10	Della - - -	7—6-10
Cynthia - - -	8—8-9	Delos - - -	10—11-8
Cyrene - - -	7—8-8	Delphi - - -	9—5-22
Cyril - - - -	4—7-6	Demosthenes - -	10—3-7
Cyrus - - -	5—10-4	Denis - - -	6—5-10
Dagmar - - -	8—2-6	Dennie - - -	6—10-5
Daisy - - - -	22—8-5	Dennis - - -	11—5-6
Dalby - - - -	8—8-9	Depew - - -	8—10-7
Dale - - - -	4—6-7	Desmond - -	11—11-9
Dalton - - -	3—7-5	Dessa - - - -	3—6-6
Damon - - -	2—7-4	Dewitt - - -	9—5-4
Dan - - -	10—1-9	Dexter - - -	4—10-3
Dana - - -	11—2-9	Diana - - -	2—11-9
Danby - - -	10—8-11	Diaz - - -	22—10-3

Dick - - - -	9—9-9	Durham - - -	11—4-7
Dickson - - -	3—6-6	Dutch - - - -	2—3-8
Dickens - - -	11—5-6	Dwight - - -	8—9-8
Disraeli - - -	5—6-8	Dyer - - - -	7—3-4
Dodge - - -	8—11-6	Earl - - - -	9—6-3
Dolly - - -	5—4-10	Earle - - -	5—11-3
Dolores - - -	7—8-8	Ed - - - -	9—5-4
Don - - - -	6—6-9	Eda - - - -	10—6-4
Donald - - -	5—7-7	Eddy - - - -	2—3-8
Dora - - - -	2—7-4	Edgar - - - -	8—6-2
Doris - - -	11—6-5	Edison - - -	3—2-10
Dorothea - - -	5—9-5	Edith - - -	10—5-5
Dorothy - -	6—10-5	Editha - - -	11—6-5
Dot - - - -	3—6-6	Edmund - - -	7—8-8
Douglas - - -	7—10-6	Edna - - - -	6—6-9
Doyle - - - -	7—9-7	Edsel - - -	9—10-8
Drake - - - -	3—6-6	Edward - -	10—6-22
Draper - - -	8—6-11	Edwin - - -	10—5-5
Drexel - - -	5—10-22	Edythe - - -	4—8-5
Drummond - -	3—9-3	Egan - - - -	9—6-3
Drusilla - - -	6—4-2	Elaine - - -	10—2-8
Dryden - - -	7—3-22	Elba - - - -	11—6-5
Duane - - -	9—9-9	Eldred - - -	3—10-2
Dudley - - -	8—8-9	Eleanor - - -	7—8-8
Duke - - - -	5—8-6	Eli - - - -	8—5-3
Dulce - - -	9—8-10	Elias - - -	10—6-4
Dumas - - -	4—4-9	Elihu - - -	10—8-11
Duncan - - -	3—4-8	Elijah - - -	9—6-3
Dunkirk - - -	7—3-22	Elisha - - - -	9—6-3
Dupont - - -	9—9-9	Elissa - - - -	2—6-5
Dupre - - -	10—8-2	Eliza - - -	8—6-11
Durand - - -	8—4-22	Elizabeth - - -	7—2-5

Name	Values		Name	Values
Ella	3—6-6		Ethelyn	8—8-9
Ellean	22—11-11		Eugene	3—9-3
Elliott	3—2-1		Eugenia	8—5-3
Ellis	3—5-7		Evan	6—6-9
Ellsworth	6—11-4		Evans	7—6-10
Elmer	8—10-7		Eva	10—6-4
Elmira	4—6-7		Eve	5—10-4
Eloise	11—7-4		Evelyn	11—8-3
Elsie	5—10-4		Everett	5—6-8
Elsworth	3—11-10		Ewing	4—5-8
Elysia	8—22-4		Ezra	5—6-8
Emanuel	8—5-3		Fairbanks	9—11-7
Emerson	8—7-10		Fairchild	7—10-6
Emery	3—8-4		Fairfax	11—11-9
Emilia	4—6-7		Faith	8—10-7
Emily	10—3-7		Fan	3—1-11
Emma	5—6-8		Fannie	4—6-7
Emmet	2—10-10		Fanny	6—8-7
Emmons	7—11-5		Farmer	7—6-10
Emory	4—9-4		Farnham	7—2-5
Enid	5—5-9		Farrar	8—2-6
Enos	8—11-6		Father	4—6-7
Ephraim	7—6-1		Fatima	5—11-3
Erastus	22—9-4		Faust	4—4-9
Eric	8—5-3		Fay	5—1-4
Erma	10—6-4		Faye	10—6-4
Ermine	10—10-9		Felice	4—10-3
Ernest	9—10-8		Felix	11—5-6
Ernestine	10—6-22		Fenwick	8—5-3
Estelle	6—6-9		Ferdinand	3—6-6
Esther	3—10-2		Ferguson	6—5-10
Ethel	5—10-4		Fern	7—5-2

Fernandez - - 3—11-10	Freda - - - 7—6-10
Finlay - - - 4—10-3	Frederick - - 7—10-6
Fischer - - - 5—5-9	Fredericka - - 8—2-6
Fisher - - - 11—5-6	Fredrick - - 11—5-6
Fisk - - - - 9—9-9	Freeman - - 8—11-6
Fiske - - - - 5—5-9	Frieda - - - 7—6-10
Fitch - - - 10—9-10	Fritz - - - - 7—9-7
Fitzgerald - - 9—6-3	Fuller - - - 11—8-3
Flavia - - - 6—11-4	Fulton - - - 7—9-7
Fleming - - - 3—5-7	Gabriel - - - 9—6-3
Fletcher - - 5—10-4	Gaby - - - - 8—8-9
Flint - - - - 7—9-7	Gaines - - - 10—6-4
Flo - - - - 6—6-9	Gail - - - 2—10-10
Flora - - - - 7—7-9	Gale - - - - 7—6-10
Florence - - - 6—7-8	Galicia - - - 6—2-4
Florian - - - 3—7-5	Garcia - - - 3—11-10
Flower - - - 7—11-5	Garden - - - 4—6-7
Floyd - - - - 8—4-4	Garibaldi - - - 9—2-7
Forbes - - - 11—11-9	Garnet - - - 11—6-5
Ford - - - - 7—6-10	Garrick - - - 4—10-3
Forrest - - - 11—11-9	Gary - - - - 6—8-7
Fortuna - - 5—10-22	Gascon - - - 5—7-7
Fortune - - - 9—5-22	Gaston - - - 22—7-6
Foster - - - 11—11-9	Gates - - - - 7—6-10
Fowler - - - 7—11-5	Gayelord - - - 6—3-3
Fox - - - - 9—6-3	Gaylord - - - 10—7-3
Frances - - - 3—6-6	Gaze - - - - 3—6-6
Francis - - - 7—10-6	Gene - - - 22—10-3
Francisca - - 11—11-9	Geneva - - - 9—11-7
Frank - - - 5—1-22	Genevieve - - 4—11-2
Franklin - - - 4—10-3	George - - - 3—7-5
Fred - - - - 6—5-10	Georgia - - - 8—3-5

Georgiana - -	5—22-10		Graves - - -	9—6-3
Georgine - -	8—7-10		Gray - - - -	6—1-5
Gerald - - -	11—6-5		Grayling - -	3—10-11
Geraldine - -	3—2-1		Green - - -	4—10-3
Gerard - - -	8—6-11		Greene - - -	9—6-3
Gerry - - -	10—3-7		Gregory - - -	5—9-5
Gertrude - - -	8—4-4		Griffith - -	11—9-11
Gibbons - - -	5—6-8		Grimes - - -	8—5-3
Gibson - - -	3—6-6		Grimm - - -	6—9-6
Gideon - - -	9—2-7		Griselda - - -	3—6-6
Gilbert - - -	10—5-5		Griswold - -	8—6-11
Giles - - -	7—5-11		Grove - - -	4—11-2
Giovanni - -	10—7-3		Grover - -	4—11-11
Giralda - - -	7—11-5		Gus - - - -	11—3-8
Gladys - - -	5—8-6		Gussie - - -	8—8-9
Gloria - - -	8—7-1		Gustavus - -	22—7-6
Glen - - - -	2—5-6		Guthrie - - -	7—8-8
Glenn - - -	7—5-2		Guy - - - -	8—10-7
Glynn - - -	9—7-2		Gwendolyn -	11—9-11
Goldie - - -	7—2-5		Hale - - -	8—6-11
Gomez - - -	3—11-10		Halifax - -	7—11-5
Good - - -	5—3-11		Hall - - - -	6—1-5
Goodwin - -	6—3-3		Hallam - - -	2—2-9
Goodyear - -	9—9-9		Hamilton - -	11—7-22
Gordon - - -	10—3-7		Hamlin - - -	3—10-2
Gould - - -	5—9-5		Hammond - -	5—7-7
Grace - - -	7—6-10		Hamon - - -	6—7-8
Gracia - - -	3—11-10		Hancock - - -	10—7-3
Graham - - -	3—2-10		Hanes - - -	2—6-5
Granger - - -	7—6-10		Hanna - - -	2—2-9
Grant - - -	6—1-5		Hannah - - -	10—2-8
Granville - -	10—6-4		Hans - - - -	6—1-5

Hansen - - - 7—6-10	Helena - - - 9—11-7
Hanson - - - 8—7-10	Helmer - - - 7—10-6
Harding - - 7—10-6	Henri - - - 9—5-22
Hardy - - - 11—8-3	Henrici - - - 3—5-7
Hargrave - - 8—7-10	Henrietta - - 10—2-8
Harlan - - - 9—2-7	Henry - - - 7—3-22
Harlow - - - 5—7-7	Herbert - - - 4—10-3
Harold - - - 4—7-6	Herman - - - 5—6-8
Harper - - - 3—6-6	Hermes - - - 5—10-4
Harriet - - - 7—6-10	Herold - - - 8—11-6
Harris - - - 10—10-9	Herring - - 7—5-11
Harrison - - - 3—7-5	Hester - - - 3—10-2
Harry - - - 7—8-8	Hezekiah - - 10—2-8
Harvey - - - 7—6-10	Hicks - - - - 5—9-5
Harwood - - - 3—4-8	Hilda - - - - 7—1-6
Hattie - - - 9—6-3	Hilde - - - 11—5-6
Hauser - - - 9—9-9	Hill - - - - 5—9-5
Hawkins - - 4—10-3	Hiram - - - 4—10-3
Hawthorne - - 4—3-10	Hobart - - - 10—7-3
Hayden - - - 3—6-6	Hobson - - - 10—3-7
Haydn - - - 7—1-6	Hoffman - - 9—7-11
Hayes - - - 22—6-7	Homer - - - 5—11-3
Haynes - - - 9—6-3	Honore - - - 3—8-22
Hays - - - - 8—1-7	Honoria - - 8—22-22
Hayward - - - 8—2-6	Hope - - - 8—11-6
Hazel - - - 7—6-10	Horace - - - 5—3-2
Hazelton - - 11—3-8	Horatio - - 5—22-10
Heath - - - 6—6-9	Hortense - - - 5—7-7
Heber - - - 11—10-10	Hosea - - - - 3—3-9
Hector - - 6—11-22	Howard - - - 6—7-8
Hedwig - - - 11—5-6	Howell - - 3—11-10
Helen - - - 8—10-7	Hubbard - - 11—4-7

Hudson - - -	9—9-9	
Hugh - - - -	8—3-5	
Hugo - - - -	6—9-6	
Hulda - - -	10—4-6	
Hume - - - -	2—8-3	
Hunt - - - -	9—3-6	
Hunter - - -	5—8-6	
Hyde - - - -	6—3-3	
Ibsen - - -	22—5-8	
Ida - - - -	5—10-4	
Ignatius - -	10—22-6	
Illinois - - -	9—6-3	
Immanuel - -	7—9-7	
Inez - - - -	9—5-4	
Ingersoll - -	3—2-10	
Iole - - - -	5—2-3	
Ione - - - -	7—2-5	
Iowa - - - -	3—7-5	
Ira - - - -	10—10-9	
Irene - - -	6—10-5	
Irvin - - - -	9—9-9	
Irving - - -	7—9-7	
Isaac - - -	6—11-4	
Isabel - - - -	3—6-6	
Isabella - - -	7—7-9	
Isabelle - - -	11—2-9	
Isadore - - -	8—3-5	
Isaiah - - -	11—2-9	
Ishmael - -	4—6-7	
Isis - - - -	2—9-2	
Israel - - -	10—6-4	
Ivan - - -	10—10-9	

Ivanhoe - -	11—3-8
Jabez - - -	8—6-11
Jack - - - -	7—1-6
Jackson - - -	10—7-3
Jacob - - - -	4—7-6
Jacqueline - -	7—5-2
Jacques - - -	22—9-4
James - - -	3—6-6
Jane - - - -	3—6-6
Janet - - - -	5—6-8
Jarvis - - -	7—10-6
Jason - - - -	5—7-7
Jean - - - -	3—6-6
Jeanette - - -	8—7-10
Jeanne - -	22—11-11
Jed - - - -	10—5-5
Jefferson - -	8—7-10
Jeffries - - -	6—10-5
Jehu - - - -	8—8-9
Jenkins - - -	10—5-5
Jennie - - -	3—10-11
Jenny - - -	5—3-11
Jeremiah - -	6—2-22
Jeremy - - -	4—8-5
Jerome - - -	3—7-5
Jerry - - - -	4—3-1
Jervis - - -	11—5-6
Jesse - - -	4—10-3
Jessica - - -	3—6-6
Jessie - - -	22—10-3
Jewel - - -	10—10-9
Joab - - - -	10—7-3

Joachim - - - 5—7-7	Juno - - - - 6—9-6
Joan - - - - 4—7-6	Jupiter - - - 9—8-10
Joanna - - - 10—8-11	Justin - - - - 3—3-9
Joanne - - - 5—3-11	Kaiser - - - 9—6-3
Joash - - - 8—7-10	Karl - - - - 6—1-5
Job - - - - 9—6-3	Karol - - - - 3—7-5
Joe - - - - 3—11-1	Kate - - - - 10—6-4
Joel - - - - 6—11-4	Katha - - - - 5—2-3
John - - - - 2—6-5	Katherine - - 10—2-8
Johnson - - - 5—3-2	Kathryn - - - 7—8-8
Johnston - - 7—3-22	Katrina - - 11—11-9
Johnstone - - 3—8-22	Keith - - - - 8—5-3
Jonah - - - - 3—7-5	Kellogg - - 6—11-22
Jonas - - - - 5—7-7	Kelly - - - - 2—3-8
Jonathan - - 11—8-3	Ken - - - - 3—5-7
Jones - - - 9—11-7	Kennedy - - - 6—8-7
Jordan - - - 8—7-10	Kenneth - - 5—10-22
Josef - - - 10—11-8	Kent - - - - 5—5-9
Joseph - - - 10—11-8	Kenyon - - 3—11-10
Josephine - - 11—7-22	Kiev - - - - 2—5-6
Josephus - - - 5—5-9	King - - - - 5—9-5
Joshua - - - 2—10-10	Kingsley - - - 3—5-7
Josiah - - - 8—7-10	Kipling - - - 6—9-6
Judah - - - 8—4-4	Kirby - - - 11—7-4
Judas - - - 10—4-6	Kirk - - - 22—9-4
Judith - - - 9—3-6	Kirke - - - 9—5-4
Judson - - - 2—9-11	Kittie - - - 11—5-6
Juel - - - - 3—8-4	Kitty - - - 22—7-6
Julia - - - - 8—4-4	Knight - - - 6—9-6
Julian - - - 22—4-9	Knox - - - 10—6-4
Julien - - - - 8—8-9	Korah - - - 8—7-10
Julius - - - 2—6-5	Krishna - - - 8—10-7

Kruger - - -	8—8-9	Letha - - - 10—6-4
Kruse - - - -	2—8-3	Levi - - - - 3—5-7
Kyrle - - -	8—3-5	Lewis - - - - 5—5-9
Lafayette - - -	5—3-2	Lille - - - - 5—5-9
Laila - - -	8—11-6	Lillian - - - 6—10-5
Lalla - - -	11—2-9	Lillie - - - - 5—5-9
Landis - - -	5—10-4	Lily - - - - 22—7-6
Larry - - -	11—8-3	Lina - - - - 9—10-8
Launce - - -	2—9-11	Lincoln - - - 7—6-10
Laura - - - -	8—5-3	Lind - - - - 3—9-3
Laurens - - -	9—9-9	Linne - - - - 9—5-4
Lawrence - -	9—11-7	Linnie - - - 9—5-4
Lea - - - -	9—6-3	Lionel - - - 4—2-11
Leah - - - -	8—6-11	Lloyd - - - 5—4-10
Lee - - - -	4—10-3	Locke - - - 10—11-8
Leigh - - -	5—5-9	Lodge - - - 7—11-5
Leighton - - -	9—2-7	Logan - - - 22—7-6
Leland - - -	3—6-6	Lois - - - - 10—6-4
Lemuel - - -	5—4-10	London - - - 11—3-8
Lena - - - -	5—6-8	Long - - - - 3—6-6
Lenna - - -	10—6-4	Loomis - - - 11—3-8
Lenora - - -	11—3-8	Lopez - - - 11—11-9
Leo - - - -	5—11-3	Loren - - - 10—11-8
Leon - - -	10—11-8	Loretta - - - 10—3-7
Leonard - - -	6—3-3	Lottie - - - - 9—2-7
Leonardo - - -	3—9-3	Lou - - - - 3—3-9
Leonidas - - -	7—3-4	Louis - - - 22—9-4
Leonore - - -	3—22-8	Louisa - - - 5—10-4
Leopold - - -	7—8-8	Louise - - - 9—5-4
Leroy - - - -	3—9-3	Lowell - - - 7—11-5
Leslie - - -	8—10-7	Lucia - - - 10—4-6
Lester - - -	7—10-6	Lucian - - - 6—4-11

Lucifer - - -	11—8-3	Margaret - - 11—7-4
Lucius - - -	22—6-7	Marguerite - - 9—5-4
Lucretia - - -	8—9-8	Maria - - - 6—11-4
Lucy - - -	7—10-6	Marian - - - 11—11-9
Ludwig - - -	4—3-10	Marianne - - - 3—7-5
Luke - - - -	4—8-5	Marie - - - 10—6-4
Lura - - - -	7—4-3	Marietta - - - 6—7-8
Luria - - - -	7—4-3	Marion - - - 7—7-9
Lydia - - - -	6—8-7	Marius - - - 9—4-5
Lynch - - -	8—7-10	Marjorie - - - 8—3-5
Lyons - - -	22—4-9	Mark - - - - 7—1-6
Lytton - - -	7—4-3	Marlow - - - 10—7-3
Macleod - - -	8—3-5	Marquette - - 3—5-7
Madden - - -	5—6-8	Marquis - - - 8—4-22
Madeline - - -	9—2-7	Marshall - - 3—2-10
Madelon - -	10—3-7	Martha - - - 7—2-5
Madison - - -	3—7-5	Martin - - - 3—10-2
Mae - - -	10—6-4	Martina - - - 4—11-2
Maggie - - -	6—6-9	Martinez - - 7—6-10
Magnus - - -	3—4-8	Martini - - - 3—10-2
Maison - - -	8—7-10	Martyn - - - 10—8-2
Major - - -	3—7-5	Marx - - - 2—1-10
Malcolm - - -	6—7-8	Mary - - - - 3—8-4
Mame - - -	5—6-8	Masie - - - - 2—6-5
Manlius - - -	8—4-4	Mason - - - 8—7-10
Manning - -	9—10-8	Mat - - - - 7—1-6
Mansfield - -	11—6-5	Mathew - - 7—6-10
Manuel - - -	3—9-3	Mathews - - - 8—6-2
Marcella - -	11—7-22	Mathias - - - 8—11-6
Marcellus - -	5—9-5	Matilda - - 6—11-4
Marcia - - -	9—11-7	Matthew - - - 9—6-3
Marcus - - -	3—4-8	Mattie - - - - 5—6-8

Maud - - - -	3—4-8	
Maude - - -	8—9-8	
Maurice - - -	7—9-7	
Max - - -	11—1-10	
Maximilian -	6—11-22	
Maxine - - -	3—6-6	
Maxwell - - -	9—6-3	
May - - - -	3—1-11	
Mayme - - -	3—6-6	
Mayo - - -	9—7-11	
Mazeppa - - -	6—7-8	
Mead - - - -	5—6-8	
Meade - - -	10—11-8	
Media - - - -	5—6-8	
Melba - - - -	6—6-9	
Melissa - - -	6—6-9	
Melita - - -	6—6-9	
Melville - -	9—10-8	
Melvin - - -	3—5-7	
Mercedes - - -	9—6-3	
Mercer - - -	8—10-7	
Meredith - -	10—10-9	
Merle - - -	8—10-7	
Merlin - - -	8—5-3	
Merton - - -	4—11-2	
Merwin - -	10—5-5	
Michael - - -	6—6-9	
Michel - - -	5—5-9	
Mike - - - -	2—5-6	
Miller - - -	6—5-10	
Millicent - - -	7—5-2	
Millie - - -	6—5-10	

Mills - - -	2—9-11	
Milton - - -	11—6-5	
Mina - - -	10—10-9	
Minerva - -	10—6-22	
Minnie - - -	10—5-5	
Mira - - -	5—10-4	
Mirabel - - -	6—6-9	
Miranda - -	6—11-22	
Miriam - - -	9—10-8	
Mirza - - -	4—10-3	
Mitzi - - - -	5—9-5	
Moab - - - -	4—7-6	
Modjeska - - -	6—3-3	
Mohammed - -	9—3-6	
Moliere - - -	5—7-7	
Mollie - - -	3—2-10	
Molly - - -	5—4-10	
Mona - - - -	7—7-9	
Monica - -	10—7-3	
Montague - -	6—6-9	
Monte - -	22—11-11	
Montgomery -	10—6-4	
Monticello - -	10—8-2	
Moody - - -	9—10-8	
Moore - - -	3—8-4	
Moran - - -	7—7-9	
Mordecai - - -	5—3-2	
Morgan - - -	5—7-7	
Morrill - - -	7—6-10	
Morris - - -	11—6-5	
Morrison - -	4—3-10	
Morse - - -	7—11-5	

Morton	- - -	5—3-2	Nemesis	- -	3—10-11
Moses	- - -	8—11-6	Neptune	- -	5—4-10
Mother	- - -	7—11-5	Nero	- - -	7—11-5
Mozart	- - -	3—7-5	Nettie	- - -	10—10-9
Muratore	- - -	3—6-6	Neva	- - - -	6—6-9
Murdock	- -	4—9-22	Neville	- - -	7—10-6
Muriel	- - -	6—8-7	Newton	- -	10—11-8
Murphy	- -	11—10-10	Nicholas	- - -	9—7-2
Myra	- - - -	3—8-4	Nichols	- - -	8—6-2
Myron	- - -	4—4-9	Nicholson	- -	10—3-7
Nada	- - -	11—2-9	Nick	- - -	10—9-10
Nadine	- - -	11—6-5	Nicol	- - -	8—6-11
Nahum	- - -	3—4-8	Nina	- - -	2—10-10
Nala	- - -	10—2-8	Nirvana	- - -	7—11-5
Nan	- - -	11—1-10	Noah	- - - -	2—7-4
Nancy	- - -	3—8-4	Noel	- - -	10—11-8
Nannie	- - -	3—6-6	Nola	- - - -	6—7-8
Naomi	- - -	7—7-9	Nona	- - -	8—7-10
Napoleon	- -	11—9-2	Nordica	- - -	10—7-3
Narcissa	- -	3—11-10	Norma	- - -	7—7-9
Natalie	- - -	8—7-10	Norman	- - -	3—7-5
Nathalie	- - -	7—7-9	Norris	- - -	3—6-6
Nathan	- - -	22—2-2	Norton	- - -	6—3-3
Nathaniel	- - -	3—7-5	Novello	- - -	5—8-6
Neal	- - - -	5—6-8	Nye	- - - -	8—3-5
Ned	- - - -	5—5-9	Nysa	- - - -	5—8-6
Neil	- - - -	22—5-8	Obadiah	- - -	4—8-5
Neiva	- - - -	6—6-9	Oberon	- - -	6—8-7
Nell	- - - -	7—5-11	O'Brien	- - -	9—2-7
Nella	- - -	8—6-11	O'Bryan	- - -	3—5-7
Nellie	- - -	3—10-11	O'Connell	- -	9—8-10
Nelson	- - -	7—11-5	O'Connor	- -	4—9-22

Octave - - -	3—3-9	
Octavia - - -	8—8-9	
Octavius - -	11—10-10	
Odessa - - -	9—3-6	
O'Donnell - -	10—8-2	
Oglesby - - -	4—9-4	
Olaf - - - -	7—7-9	
Ole - - - -	5—11-3	
Olga - - -	8—7-10	
Olin - - - -	5—6-8	
Oliva - - - -	5—7-7	
Olive - - - -	9—2-7	
Oliver - - -	9—2-7	
Olivia - - -	5—7-7	
Oman - - -	7—7-9	
Omar - - - -	2—7-4	
Omer - - -	6—11-4	
Ona - - - -	3—7-5	
O'Neil - - -	10—2-8	
Ora - - - -	7—7-9	
Orel - - -	5—11-3	
Orlando - - -	7—4-3	
Orleans - - -	3—3-9	
Orloff - - -	9—3-6	
Orpheus - - -	3—5-7	
Orville - - -	3—2-10	
Oscar - - - -	2—7-4	
Osgood - - -	3—9-3	
Oswald - - -	2—7-4	
Otho - - -	22—3-10	
Otis - - - -	9—6-3	
Otto - - - -	7—3-4	

Owen - - -	3—11-10
Page - - - -	2—6-5
Paine - - - -	9—6-3
Palmer - - -	11—6-5
Pamela - - -	3—7-5
Panches - - -	3—6-6
Pancho - - -	3—7-5
Pandora - - -	6—8-7
Park - - -	10—1-9
Parker - - -	6—6-9
Parry - - - -	6—8-7
Pascal - - - -	7—2-5
Paterson - - -	9—3-6
Patterson - -	11—3-8
Patti - - -	3—10-11
Patton - - -	5—7-7
Paul - - - -	5—4-10
Paula - - -	6—5-10
Paulina - - -	11—5-6
Pauline - - -	6—9-6
Pavia - - -	22—11-11
Payne - - -	7—6-10
Pearl - - -	7—6-10
Pedro - - -	4—11-2
Pembroke - - -	4—7-6
Penn - - - -	22—5-8
Pepys - - - -	9—3-6
Percival - - -	5—6-8
Percy - - -	4—3-10
Perkins - - -	11—5-6
Perry - - -	10—3-7
Peter - - -	10—10-9

Reeves - - -	11—6-5	
Regan - - -	9—6-3	
Reggie - - -	6—10-5	
Reggio - - -	7—2-5	
Regina - - -	9—6-3	
Reid - - - -	9—5-4	
Reinhart - - -	3—6-6	
Rembrandt - -	5—6-8	
Remus - - -	22—8-5	
Rene - - -	6—10-5	
Reno - - -	7—11-5	
Reuben - - -	11—4-7	
Reva - - -	10—6-4	
Reynolds - -	4—11-11	
Rhea - - - -	5—6-8	
Rhodes - - -	6—11-22	
Richard - - -	7—10-6	
Richelieu - - -	9—4-5	
Ring - - - -	3—9-3	
Robert - -	6—11-22	
Roberta - - -	7—3-22	
Roberts - - -	7—11-5	
Robins - - -	5—6-8	
Robinson - -	7—3-22	
Robson - - -	11—3-8	
Roderick - -	11—2-9	
Roderigo - -	10—8-11	
Rodgers - - -	5—11-3	
Rodin - - - -	6—6-9	
Rodriguez - -	6—5-10	
Roger - - -	9—11-7	
Roland - - -	10—7-3	

Rolfe - - -	11—11-9	
Rolla - - -	22—7-6	
Rolle - - -	8—11-6	
Rollo - - - -	9—3-6	
Roman - - -	7—7-9	
Romeo - - -	3—8-4	
Romulus - -	11—3-8	
Roosevelt - -	5—22-10	
Rosa - - -	8—7-10	
Rosalie - - -	7—3-4	
Rosalind - -	11—7-22	
Rosaline - - -	3—3-9	
Rosamond - -	9—4-5	
Roscoe - - -	3—8-4	
Rose - - -	3—11-10	
Rosetta - - -	8—3-5	
Rosini - - -	3—6-6	
Ross - - - -	8—6-11	
Roth - - -	7—6-10	
Roxana - - -	10—8-2	
Roy - - - -	22—4-9	
Ruben - - -	6—8-7	
Rudolf - -	4—9-22	
Rudolph - - -	4—9-4	
Rupert - - -	8—8-9	
Ruskin - - -	11—3-8	
Russell - - -	7—8-8	
Ruth - - -	22—3-10	
Rutherford - -	7—5-11	
Ryan - - -	22—8-5	
Sade - - - -	11—6-5	
Sadie - - - -	2—6-5	

Sadler - - - -	5—6-8	Shelby - - - 8—3-5
Salina - - -	2—11-9	Sheldon - - - 5—11-3
Salome - - -	2—3-8	Sheridan - - - 6—6-9
Sam - - - -	6—1-5	Sherman - - - 6—6-9
Sambo - - -	5—7-7	Silvester - - - 3—10-2
Samson - - -	9—7-11	Silvia - - - 9—10-8
Samuel - - -	8—9-8	Simon - - - 7—6-10
Sancho - - -	6—7-8	Simpson - - - 6—6-9
Sandford - -	9—7-11	Sloan - - - - 7—7-9
Sando - - -	8—7-10	Sloane - - - 3—3-9
Sandy - - -	9—8-10	Smith - - - - 6—9-6
Sanford - - -	5—7-7	Smyth - - - 22—7-6
Sappho - - -	3—7-5	Sofia - - - - 5—7-7
Sara - - - -	3—2-10	Solomon - - - 4—9-4
Sarah - - - -	2—2-9	Sophia - - - - 5—7-7
Sargent - - -	3—6-6	Sophie - - - 9—2-7
Sari - - -	2—10-10	Sophronia - - 7—22-3
Saul - - - -	8—4-4	Sousa - - - 3—10-2
Saunders - -	11—9-2	Spence - - - 8—10-7
Scot - - - -	3—6-6	Sprague - - - 6—9-6
Scott - - - -	5—6-8	Stanley - - - 6—6-9
Sebastian - -	9—7-11	Stella - - - - 6—6-9
Selina - - - -	6—6-9	Stephen - - - 6—10-5
Selma - - - -	5—6-8	Stephens - - 7—10-6
Selwyn - - -	8—3-5	Steve - - - 8—10-7
Sergius - - -	8—8-9	Steven - - - 22—10-3
Seth - - - -	7—5-11	Stevens - - - 5—10-4
Seton - - -	10—11-8	Sterling - - - 5—5-9
Seward - - -	7—6-10	Stewart - - - 7—6-10
Shakespeare - -	9—8-10	Stokes - - - 8—11-6
Sharp - - - -	8—1-7	Stone - - - 10—11-8
Sheba - - -	8—6-11	Stuart - - - - 9—4-5

Sue - - - - 9—8-1	Timothy - - 11—22-7
Sullivan - - - 11—4-7	Tindal - - - 6—10-5
Sumner - - - 9—8-10	Todd - - - 7—6-10
Susan - - - 11—4-7	Tolstoi - - - 11—3-8
Susie - - - 10—8-2	Tom - - - - 3—6-6
Suzanne - - 10—9-10	Tommy - - 5—4-10
Sylvester - - 10—8-2	Tompkins - - 9—6-3
Sylvia - - - - 7—8-8	Topsy - - - 5—4-10
Tabitha - - - 7—11-5	Tracy - - - 22—8-5
Tacie - - - - 2—6-5	Trent - - - - 5—5-9
Tad - - - - 7—1-6	Trilby - - - 5—7-7
Taft - - - 11—1-10	Tucker - - - 6—8-7
Talmage - - - 5—7-7	Tyler - - - - 8—3-5
Ted - - - - 11—5-6	Tyndall - - - 7—8-8
Terry - - - - 5—3-2	Tyrol - - - 9—4-5
Texas - - - 6—6-9	Ulrich - - - 8—3-5
Thaddeus - - 10—9-10	Underwood - - 11—2-9
Thais - - - 3—10-11	Upton - - - 5—9-5
Thalia - - - 6—11-4	Uranus - - - 22—7-6
Thanet - - - 5—6-8	Uriel - - - 11—8-3
Thelma - - - 5—6-8	Ursula - - - 2—7-4
Theodora - - - 5—9-5	Valentine - - 3—2-10
Theodore - - 9—22-5	Valeria - - - 5—7-7
Theresa - - - 4—11-2	Valla - - - 3—2-10
Theron - - - 8—11-6	Vanderbilt - - 8—6-11
Thirza - - 10—10-9	Vandyke - - 10—4-6
Thomas - - - 22—7-6	Venus - - - 9—8-10
Thora - - - 8—7-10	Vera - - - 10—6-4
Thoreau - - 7—6-10	Verden - - 5—10-22
Thurston - - - 9—9-9	Verdie - - - 9—10-8
Tibbie - - - 11—5-6	Vergil - - - 10—5-5
Tillie - - - - 4—5-8	Vern - - - - 5—5-9

Name	Value	Name	Value
Verna	6—6-9	Washington	4—7-6
Verne	10—10-9	Watts	11—1-10
Vernon	7—11-5	Waverly	7—4-3
Verona	3—3-9	Wayland	8—2-6
Veronica	6—3-3	Webster	11—10-10
Vesta	4—6-7	Wellington	5—2-3
Victor	6—6-9	Wells	8—5-3
Victoria	7—7-9	Wesley	8—10-7
Violet	11—2-9	West	4—5-8
Virgil	5—9-5	Whalen	9—6-3
Virginia	8—10-7	Wheeler	4—6-7
Vishnu	3—3-9	White	11—5-6
Vivian	5—10-4	Whitman	7—10-6
Volga	3—7-5	Whyte	9—3-6
Voltaire	3—3-9	Wilber	6—5-10
Vonda	2—7-4	Wilbur	4—3-10
Vondel	9—11-7	Wilhelm	10—5-5
Wade	6—6-9	Wilhelmina	7—6-10
Wagner	5—6-8	Wilkes	7—5-11
Waldemar	5—7-7	Wilkins	7—9-7
Walden	5—6-8	William	7—10-6
Waldo	10—7-3	Williams	8—10-7
Walker	7—6-10	Willis	3—9-3
Wallace	3—7-5	Wilma	22—10-3
Waller	8—6-2	Wilson	11—6-5
Walsh	9—1-8	Winifred	7—5-11
Walter	7—6-10	Winnie	11—5-6
Wanamaker	6—8-7	Winslow	7—6-10
Ward	10—1-9	Winston	6—6-9
Warfield	6—6-9	Winthrop	6—6-9
Warner	7—6-10	Wright	4—9-4
Warren	7—6-10	Xanthippe	5—6-8

Xaver - - -	7—6-10	
Xavier - - -	7—6-10	
Xenia - - -	8—6-11	
Xenophon - -	3—8-4	
Xerxes - - -	5—10-22	
Yates - - -	7—6-10	
York - - - -	6—6-9	
Young - - -	10—9-10	
Yvette - - -	7—8-8	
Yvon - - -	22—4-9	
Yvonne - - -	5—9-5	
Zaccheus - - -	5—9-5	
Zachariah - -	3—3-9	
Zacharias - -	5—3-11	
Zadok - - -	3—7-5	
Zella - - - -	2—6-5	
Zeno - - - -	6—11-4	
Zenobia - - -	9—3-6	
Zephon - -	3—11-10	
Zephyr - - -	8—3-5	
Zerlina - - -	4—6-7	
Zeus - - - -	8—8-9	
Zollner - -	3—11-10	
Zora - - - -	6—7-8	

PRIVATE READINGS

THE author will be glad to assist you in the adjustment of your individual problems on receipt of the following information in your own handwriting:

Full name as given at birth.

Present name among family and friends.

Business signature.

Birth date—month, day and year.

If vocational guidance is desired, give education and previous lines followed in order that we may help you to cash in on your present assets.

Complete analysis, with adjustment of name and business signature, $10.00. Send in as many questions as you desire.

ADVANCED COURSE

Finding Yourself Through Numbers has been prepared by the author for those who desire to go deeper into the subject. It gives specific directions for charting a name, for vocational guidance, business building, selling, aids to the health, teaching and professional work, yearly influences, and an extensive list of famous people who bear out the proof of numbers in their birth date and name. A detailed outline of the course will be mailed free upon receipt of full name and birth date.

NUMEROLOGICAL GUIDE

Your *"Personal Calendar of Lucky Days"* for the entire year, with your *Personal Colors*, prepared for you upon receipt of your birthday, month, day and year. Price 50c.

ARIEL YVON TAYLOR
310 Riverside Drive at 103rd St.
Roerich Museum Bldg.
New York City